# moving
# beyond
# racism

# moving beyond racism:

memories, transformations and the
start of new conversations

edited by

heather powers albanesi
and
carole ann camp

White
River
Press

Moving Beyond Racism

Edited by Heather Powers Albanesi and Carole Ann Camp

Published 2008 by White River Press

Cover image "Yellow Leaves" © 2008 by JC Davis
www.JCDavisPhotos.com

White River Press
PO Box 4624
White River Junction, VT 05001
www.WhiteRiverPress.com

ISBN: 978-1-935052-11-1

Library of Congress Cataloging-in-Publication Data
Moving beyond racism : memories, transformations, and the start of new
conversations / edited by Heather Albanesi and Carole Ann Camp.
    p. cm.
  ISBN 978-1-935052-11-1 (pbk. : alk. paper)
    1.   United States—Race relations. 2.   Racism—United States.   I.
Albanesi, Heather, 1969- II. Camp, Carole Ann.
  E184.A1M75 2008
  305.800973--dc22
                                        2008042931

# dedication

In honor of the
Reverend Dr. Jeremiah Wright
And in memory of Valerie Russell

Experience, in whatever sphere of life it comes, is best followed by conversation. Conversation, conflicting interpretations, can lead to convictions about what is good for living in this world. Commitment to act on those convictions is what it means to be Christian.

This collection is about life experiences which have led to change. Read. . . converse. . . convict. . . commit. . . "moving beyond racism" is possible.

—Horace Seldon, founder of
Commmunity Change, Inc.

# Contents

## Transformations

## The Start of New Conversations

# introduction

During the spring of 2008, one of the media's feeding frenzies involved a United Church of Christ congregation in Chicago, pastored by the Reverend Dr. Jeremiah Wright. For days and weeks, all one could see on every news channel were a few very short clips, absent of context, of Reverend Wright's sermons preached some time ago. What followed outraged many on both sides of the political fence. The sound bites lent themselves to commentators' easy, negative analysis of the sermons. In the traditional media, commentators offered an interpretation, couched in the language of patriotism, that Wright was too angry, that he overstated the problem of racism in America today.

While some were extremely frustrated at this nearly universal take on Wright's sermons and felt it served to mask the continuing reality of racial oppression, others saw a positive side, in that racism had resurfaced as a topic of conversation in homes across America. Nearly forty years after the Civil Rights Movement had "fixed everything," people started talking, discussing, and even arguing about racism in the United States. Was racism still with us? If so, how could that be after such a long period of time? Or had racism just changed from blatant, in-your-face discrimination to a new, post-affirmative action, "color-blind" racism.

The success of Barack Obama in securing the Democratic nomination for president has also resulted in a dizzying array of effects on Americans' perceptions of the race issue. The February 25th cover of *U.S. News & World Report* featured a close-up photo of Obama along with the question "Does Race Still Matter?" The juxtaposition of the two makes the question seem rhetorical because the reader is almost forced to conclude that if Obama has made it this far in the presidential contest, then race must not matter.

But Obama's success can alternatively be read as a clear illustration of what sociologist Patricia Hill Collins labels the new racism. According to Collins, the way that class intersects with race today allows us to think race is no longer relevant. In sharp contrast to 60 years ago, a significant number of African Americans are (more or less) safely secured in the professional or upper middle-class. The existence of this group has reshaped mainstream America's perception of race, making it possible for the discrimination against poor and working-class African Americans to continue. To the extent that middle-class whites identify with and include middle-class blacks in their social and professional worlds or embrace celebrities like Tiger Woods and Oprah Winfrey, they perceive themselves as colorblind and believe that racism is dead.

Yet the personal and institutional exclusion of poor and working class blacks continues, and Collins' conception of the new racism focuses on this. African Americans living in poverty are incorrectly assumed to have a different set of values than middle class Americans, and it is these dysfunctional values that are to blame for this group not escaping poverty.

Collins also demonstrates how this new racism also constrains the black professional class because the acceptable path to economic success requires a certain deference to the white establishment. As Michael Grunwald reflects, "White America already embraces black celebrities, even 'flashy' ones. But it has never really warmed up to an angry one." (September 15, 2008, www.time.com)

Obama's appeal to white Americans requires a similar capitulation to these rules. Any mention of the issue of racism is made at the risk of being accused of "playing the race card." As a silencing technique, the "race card" expression so loved by political pundits is extremely effective.

In the midst of this reawakened (yet ambivalent) awareness of the issue of race, a number of churches decided to enter the discussion. The United Church of Christ at all levels of structure, along with the National Council of Churches, decided to take this moment in history as an opportunity to revisit the issue of racism and all of its ramifications, for all peoples, regardless of the shade of their skin, the shape of their eyes, or the color of their hair.

May 18th, 2008 was declared to be a day of "Sacred Conversations on Race." Clergy were invited to preach on the topic and members of congregations were encouraged to talk to each other about racism. The churches responded. Clergy preached sermons. Small groups gathered before, during, and after worship to share stories. Associations, conferences, and other judicatories of the United Church of Christ sent pastoral letters to all their member churches, prepared worship and workshop materials for congregations, and racism was cracked open again for all to see.

Following the sermon at the First Congregational Church in Amherst, Massachusetts, UCC, people in small groups began the process of sharing their stories. As a result of the sharing, this book, *Moving Beyond Racism: Memories, Transformations, and the Start of New Conversations* took root.

A few of the sermons preached on May 18th are included in these pages, but this is really a book of stories, a collection of people's personal memories, feelings, experiences, and reflections. The contributors to this book are not professional writers. For several, this is the first time they have been published. To begin their writing career with such a topic as racism took some courage and encouragement. It's not that easy to go public with one's feelings about racism. We thank all who sent us their stories. We also appreciate all who told us their stories but were not quite ready to share them with the world.

Many moments of insight came to those who started to write. One person cried for days. One person, after decades, finally talked to his mother about racism. Several people discovered buried feelings they didn't know they had, and were embarrassed to discover.

We share our stories with you in the hope that you will begin to share your stories with others, to keep this conversation going. If we ever have the hope of moving beyond racism, we have to look deeply into our own hearts, and bring our memories, experiences, feelings, hurts, understandings, and transformations into the light.

*—Dr. Heather Powers Albanesi, PhD.*
*—The Rev. Dr. Carole Ann Camp*

memories

# we are not afraid

## dusty miller

The first time I met Geraldine Johnson, I was scared. She was a big woman, muscular, forceful, and she seemed to be angry. The morning we met, I was sitting on the porch of the little cabin where I lived for the summer with Vicey and Elijah Walls, an elderly African-American couple. It was the summer of 1964 and I had recently arrived in West Tennessee to offer up my 19-year-old, white self as a civil rights worker. Mama and Daddy Walls were among the brave cadre of black sharecroppers who dared to share their homes with us Northern college students there for the summer to help organize voter registration.

I had only been in Fayette County for a few weeks when Geraldine Johnson pulled up in a cloud of red dust and jumped out of her dilapidated truck. Her face was stern and her deep voice chilled me. "You'all got my Jack?" she asked me in a challenging tone.

There was a silence while I stared at her, uncomprehending. Did she think I had kidnapped a child? Or was she accusing me of stealing her husband? I had never met Geraldine before, but this was exactly the kind of moment that kept recurring—people asking me things, telling me things, offering me cold drinks and food while I struggled to understand what was being said. I might as well have been a Peace Corps worker trying to understand Urdu.

That particular morning, I was hitting bottom. I was hot, dust-coated, and sleep-deprived. The other college student who shared my quarters at the Walls' was a fidgety sleeper who ground her teeth all night. We were both afraid to go to the outhouse alone after dark, so we were up and down at night accompanying each other through the sultry darkness, flashlights poised to catch the glint of spiders and other terrifying life forms in the dark little wooden structure.

The night before, I had been seated over the hole when my flashlight caught the unmistakable red hourglass of a Black Widow spider dangling inches from my face. I leaped off the outhouse bench mid-stream, and burst through the door to announce my discovery to Margie who was waiting outside for her turn. She inspected the spider-without stepping through the outhouse door-confirming my entomological assessment. After calmly squatting to pee where she stood, she announced firmly "We have to wake up Mama Walls and tell her. One of them could get bitten."

We marched resolutely back into the house, and Margie knocked on the thin door separating their bedroom from the small kitchen, the only other room in the house besides our little bedroom.

"What?" Mama Walls growled irritably. Daddy Walls kept on snoring.

"There's a Black Widow in the outhouse!" Margie announced excitedly, thrilled to be the bearer of this alarming news.

Mama Walls heaved herself upright in bed and lit the kerosene lamp. "Say what?" she asked, staring at us as if we were ghosts.

"A Black Widow! In the outhouse!" I echoed Margie in a shrill whisper.

"Who?" Mama Walls demanded incredulously. "Who you say in my outhouse?" She was probably wishing she had never offered her home to these bizarre young white visitors from the North.

We spoke simultaneously. "It's a Black Widow spider, very poisonous. We wanted to warn you so you wouldn't get bitten."

Mama Walls slowly got herself up and out of the bed, and walked painfully into the kitchen where we had retreated nervously. "Show me what you talkin' 'bout," she ordered, leading the way to the outhouse with her kerosene lantern held high.

When we showed her the spider, she sighted wearily. "That just a little old spider," she said dismissively. "Always be there. Won't do you no harm."

We spent some time trying to convince both of the Walls that the spider in the outhouse was truly dangerous, but they simply shrugged it off. Daddy Walls even giggled a little and pulled his hat brim down, perhaps to hide his amusement at our Northern squeamishness.

Now, in the light of morning, I was facing an angry black woman accusing me of harboring Jack, whoever he was.

"I don't know what you mean," I said nervously. "I don't even know who Jack is."

Geraldine stared at me, then erupted in a mighty burst of laughter. "My truck jack," she explained after she finished laughing. "Your man Danny, he borrowed my truck jack last week and now my husband Howard, he need the jack to fix a flat." She walked over to the porch and looked me in the eye. "I'm Geraldine Johnson and I live with my kids and my husband Howard over on the second road off the black top near Cavalry Baptist."

I came down off the porch to shake her hand. "I don't know if Danny has your jack or not," I said apologetically. "He's not my partner, he's Margie's. And they've already left for the day. They're going into Memphis to try to get their car repaired, I think."

"What you doing today?" Geraldine inquired, now as friendly as she had seemed angry a few minutes ago.

"Just waiting for Paul to come pick me up," I said. "He's my partner."

"You'all married?" Geraldine asked, a routine question I was beginning to recognize even after a few weeks here.

"Oh no, no, no, definitely not," I answered, shuddering. I could barely tolerate my summer work partner, a boy my age who was twice as nervous as I and more hindrance than help so far.

Geraldine laughed another great roaring laugh. "Forget the man," she advised. "You want to come over and meet my kids and I'll fix you up some chicken and biscuits for breakfast?" I hopped into her truck without a second thought, about to begin one of the most transformative friendships of my life.

As the summer wore on, I gradually began to understand more of what was going on around me. I became more comfortable with the differences in southern black and northern white ways of speaking and ways of living. I began to understand that the presence of a poisonous spider in the outhouse was a minor inconvenience compared to the daily danger and suffering most residents of Fayette County were accustomed to. I learned that someone like Geraldine could appear to be fierce and bold, and be quivering with fear inside just like me. I also discovered that the presence of young white students like me was both welcome and dangerous for everyone who associated with us. On the one hand, we drew national attention to the civil rights movement sweeping the South, thus making it a little safer for African Americans to participate in civil rights and civil disobedience because of the public spotlight shining on all of us. On the other hand, we brought increased danger to our hosts as southern whites felt increasingly threatened and outraged by our presence.

I also knew that suddenly I was on a very big adventure that would change my own life immeasurably. My world was expanding in ways I could not have named at that time, although I could sense that my eyes and my heart were opening very wide. I certainly didn't realize back in 1964 that all of us college students were receiving far more than we could possibly give.

When I contemplate those Freedom Summers, now filed away volumes ago in my memory, I'm flooded with gratitude for what I learned from Geraldine Johnson and her neighbors. I had arrived there scarred and scattered from a childhood marked by violation and emotional neglect. I had no faith in anything at nineteen, mistrusting family, school, and community. I felt hopeless about my fate as a female in a culture where men appeared to hold all the cards. I had no idea that I could successfully challenge the legacy of victimhood that seemed to doom me.

Geraldine was my master teacher, although I had hundreds of role models around me in the South, inspiring me with their courage and faith. Geraldine taught me how to be a woman who could stand up to men. I got to know her well enough eventually to know that she was scared at times, vulnerable not only as a woman but because she was also poor and black. Yet time and again I witnessed her speaking truth to power. Night after night, in each little rural church where we gathered to spread the word about voter rights, I listened to Geraldine's strong deep voice urging her neighbors to risk their lives and their children's lives for the cause of freedom. When we joined hands at the end of the meeting, sweat-drenched and exhausted, I felt the power of our voices singing "We are not afraid."

At the end of the first summer, I had no idea if I would be returning to Fayette County or not. It was a relief to be heading back to my comfortable white life as a college student, but my heart was heavy as I said my goodbyes. The most painful ending was the moment when I had to say goodbye to Geraldine.

"You better come back down here, girl!" she commanded me. "You better not go back up North and forget about us, or I'm gonna have to come up there and carry you back myself and you know this old truck can't hardly get all that way."

"I'll be back," I answered, not knowing at the time that I was telling the truth.

She grabbed me in a big warm hug. "I love you," she told me, her heart as open as her clear brown eyes. In this moment I learned about unconditional love, something that I had never before experienced.

"I love you too," I said, letting my tears flow into hers.

# don't touch

## kimberley broderick

"Your boy has such beautiful, curly hair."

"Thank you," I replied with a smile to the white woman standing next to me.

"He must not be all black. I've never seen a black person with hair like that before. Can I touch his hair?"

My son and I were grocery shopping at the Bread and Circus near our town. David, who was three years old at the time, was sitting in the seat in the cart. We were trapped in the butter, cheese and eggs aisle. I wasn't the only one looking for lactose-free cheese for their child.

I looked at this woman, not believing what I had just heard. I couldn't believe she had said to me, "He must not be all black." Touch his hair? I thought, are you crazy! You probably don't even know any black people.

I was glaring at her now, studying her. She looked to be about my age, in her early forties with brownish-red hair, probably dyed. She wore a blue-patterned, sleeveless summer dress. I noticed that her forearms were heavily freckled, and on her feet she wore Birkenstocks.

"No, you can't touch his hair," I said, barely hiding the anger that was threatening to erupt.

"I just want to touch it," she said, grinning as she stretched out her arm and hand to do just that.

I was stuck between the refrigerated cheese and this woman. I couldn't go forward because there was someone in front of me, and she was to my right. I felt trapped.

In a louder voice, I said, "No, you cannot touch his hair." Other shoppers turned to look at us.

David was staring at me. I knew he could feel my anger. "It's okay," I said to him, "Mama's not mad at you." He knitted his brow into a frown and pushed out his little lips. The woman now actually moved closer to us and had the nerve to glare at me!

"I just want to touch his hair. It looks so soft."

And it was soft. He had silky hair like my grandmother and my sister. I loved running my fingers through his hair and looking at his face that reflected the entirety of his heritage in one tiny perfect oval— African, Native American, Jamaican, Irish, Russian-Jewish, and French.

I sighed heavily, amazed that this kind of shit still happened, angry that it was happening in front of David, and a little embarrassed that people were looking at us. I felt as though I had done something wrong but at the same time I couldn't believe the audacity of this woman. Not only did she insist on touching my son, but she felt she had the right to do so.

"You can't touch his hair," I replied firmly. "Slavery ended a long time ago and if I say you can't touch him, then you can't touch him. Now, please, move out of my way."

"I...I wasn't implying anything! How can you say that?" she said, stumbling over her words as a slight blush appeared on her face.

And then, she did it again, she reached out her hand to touch my son and I, as any good mother would do when a child is about to do something dangerous, slapped her hand.

"You, you slapped me, you assaulted me." Now, she was angry and the redness in her face was not from embarrassment.

"I—assaulted you?" I yelled loudly. "What do you call what you've been doing to me and my son? You assaulted me, lady." The volcano inside me was near to overflow, and my don't-embarrass-the-white-people-when-they're-being-stupid valve popped off under the pressure and hit the ceiling. I walked toward her, leaving David and the cart behind me. "What makes you think you can just 'touch his hair?' He's not your child, you don't know us and yet you think you have the right to touch him. Why? Because you, white woman, can just do what you want? Oh no, not this time! You can mess with me, but not with my child."

"I'm calling the police," she said in a shaky voice. She was scared now. She'd awakened something she couldn't handle.

"Go ahead, call the police. I wish you would call the police. You can't just go around trying to touch children. You wanna call the police, go ahead!" I could feel my heart pumping in my chest, feel the anger seething in my veins as I stood before her not thinking, just feeling sick of it all. All I'd wanted to do was go grocery shopping.

At the sound of my angry yelling, two store employees came scurrying over to us. I picked up David out of the cart. His body was rigid with fear and his face was all scrunched up.

I rubbed his back as I explained to one of the employees what had happened. I don't know where the woman went nor did I care. I took David to the in-store café for a snack and to calm myself down. People were looking at me, but no one said a word.

After our snack, I retrieved my cart, plunked David down in the seat and headed for the checkout. I was exhausted and my body was sore from being so tense. I started putting my items on the belt when I noticed that David had lifted his shirt and was looking at his belly. Distractedly, I asked him what he was doing.

"Mama, that lady was wrong. I'm not black anywhere. I'm brown all over, even on my belly."

I shook my head and laughed out loud.

# good intentions

## carole ann camp

About forty years ago, my husband and I had two toddlers. My husband taught in the local high school, I was a "stay-at-home" mom. In those days, we were living the life of the ideal American family! My younger daughter even had blond hair and blue eyes.

The church we attended had founded an A Better Chance (ABC) house in our town. The idea behind this program was to take boys with "potential" who attended poor inner city schools and give them an opportunity to attend really good schools and enhance their chances of success. In the 1960s, this seemed like a terrific idea!

There was a board of directors for the program that oversaw all of the ins and outs of getting a dozen young men from here and there around the country to our town. The board oversaw the maintenance of the house and the financing needed for the daily needs of the students. They also hired a resident director and a cook.

My husband and I and our two children were asked to serve as the resident family for the house. We were chosen because we were "perfect." As one of the board members said, "You will be an ideal role model for these boys. They need to see what a real family is."

We were incredibly flattered even though neither my husband nor I had had much contact with people of other races or ethnic groups. Some of my husband's ancestors had even come to Massachusetts on the Mayflower, for heaven's sake. But with absolutely good intentions and all the naiveté of twenty-something white Yankees, we accepted the position.

When we started, we had no idea what racism really was and the subtle ways that it manifested itself in every minute of every day. Neither did we know that the board of directors had replaced the single, African-American young man who had been the resident director the previous year with our family because, with all their mixed-up good intentions, the board members believed we were a better role model than he was. After all, we were married, had two perfect children, my husband was deeply respected in the community, we were good Christian people, and we were stable. We were also as white as snow and knew nothing about the lives of the young men coming to live at the ABC House. The former director, on the other hand, was single, black, street-wise, and knew something of the young men's life experience. When I think back on it, I want to throw up. Good intentions. UGH!

The board of directors also hired an inexperienced white cook who prepared his nice meals with my help. But when the food was placed on the tables, the young men looked at it, looked at each other, and almost went on a hunger strike. Trying to bring some order out of the chaos, John (the cook) and I tried to solicit suggestions for meals that the young men would like. I had never heard the word chitlins before and had never seen a collard green. Neither had John. We were thinking "tuna noodle casserole and apple pie." Good intentions. UGH!

On another occasion, one of the board members said, "I'm so glad you are here, now you will be able to get them to do their laundry once a week." Good intentions. UGH!

One day, I came home and there was a pile of junk on the front porch, I could hardly get through the door. I asked one of the young men, what all that stuff was. He said, "Didn't you know? People leave that stuff on our porch instead of taking it to the dump." Good intentions. UGH!

Nothing was going right or well. The young men were getting more and more frustrated, I was getting more and more scared, and my husband looked like he was going to have a nervous breakdown. After all, he's one of the good guys, and he was trying with all his love and effort to make this work, but it wasn't working.

One image that sticks in my head is having a "conversation" with one of the young men. He was trying to explain to me what was wrong. I was listening intently, but I didn't understand a thing. His mouth was moving, sounds and words were coming out, but somewhere between him and me was an impenetrable, invisible wall. I just plain did not understand anything he was saying. In my head, I had thoughts like, "What's wrong with tuna noodle doodle?" "What's wrong with going to bed at a 'decent' hour like nine o'clock or at the very latest, ten o'clock on school nights?" "But it's not polite to wear your hat inside a building!" "What's wrong with Prell shampoo?" (In those days, there wasn't one appropriate hair product available within 25 miles of our town for a dozen African-American teenagers.)

Eventually, some good came from this incredibly painful few months. We got fired! Unfortunately, we got fired to save us, not the young men in the ABC program. Fortunately, however, the board of directors replaced us with the previous resident director which turned out to be a very good thing.

The other plus that came from our good-intentions-gone-awry was an invitation to take a six-month intensive, anti-racism training course conducted by Community Change, Inc. of Boston and led by Horace Seldon. My husband and I had our world-view changed. Un-learning racism is a life-long, and at times, very difficult process.

# blinded by the white

## maxine philips

It wasn't the first time I'd seen white privilege, but it was the beginning of my understanding of it. On a cold, clear, late winter day almost forty years ago, I was in a rally in front of New York's City Hall to protest the lack of decent housing for welfare recipients. It was supposed to be a spirited rally that, we hoped, would make the news. But when George Wiley, the charismatic head of the National Welfare Rights Organization (NWRO), called for volunteers to take over an unoccupied middle income housing complex on the Upper West Side, I headed toward the waiting bus. It wasn't the day I'd planned.

We made the news all right. My friends got a kick out of my raised-fist salute on TV as we were herded out of the building and onto the police vans. What they didn't see was what happened next. Forty women, two of us white, the rest African-American, were put in a large, dreary room at the West 100th Street precinct house. The four men—two black, two white—were put in cells.

After a few hours, the white guys appeared, joking about the fleas they'd acquired while sitting on the beds. The black ones, NWRO staffers, were being processed, we assumed. Suddenly one of them, Gary, landed, literally, at my feet, thrown into the group by a police officer who thought he'd been too slow to stand up when told to move. Then the second NWRO staffer was hurled into the holding room. Both were still handcuffed, and as the police pummeled them on the floor, Gary's glasses flew across the floor.

It was over quickly as others pulled the police off and our pro bono lawyers immediately started negotiating. If they do this in broad daylight, in front of lawyers, what goes on when there are no witnesses? I thought.

The lawyers worked hard to be sure the two weren't charged with attacking a police officer, and they succeeded. The women were still there. I'd already used my one phone call to tell my boss I wouldn't be back, but I was starting to worry about the next day. The lawyers moved through our group, taking down our information.

"When can I leave?"

"What were you charged with?"

"I don't know."

"You mean nobody booked you?"

If I hadn't been booked, he grinned, then I should try to leave. Sure enough, my arresting officer had gone home hours before. Technically, I was a free woman. Returning to the group gathered around the table where I'd been sitting, I said good-by and expressed my bewilderment. After all, I was thinking, although I didn't say it, I sort of stood out. How could I have been overlooked?

Ten African-American women looked at me in my business clothes. One smiled. "Honey, you look like a social worker. They musta figured you didn't belong with us."

# naming racism: what would you do?

## marylou sullivan

I am a single white woman who adopted two multi-racial children. My older son, Dan, was born in Brazil. He came to me through a connection my brother had with a family in Brazil as a result of a student exchange. I hadn't been pursuing international adoption, but my brother saw my frustration and disappointment in trying to adopt locally and he reached out on my behalf. Six years later, I adopted Matt here in the states. I had been reaching out for siblings, school-age girls, but providence brought me infant boys six years apart. They are the wonder and joy of my life.

The stories about both adoptions are rich with the interplay of choices and fate, but they are not the subject here. I want to share a story that was a painful incident in my life, in our family life, and one that still raises more questions than answers.

It was Columbus Day, 1996. The weather was perfect. My older son Dan, then eight, was out in the neighborhood playing with friends. His brother, Matt, twenty months old, was sleeping. There was a knock at my door, and an older woman with little girl with blond hair stood on my doorstep. As soon as I answered the door, the woman began shaking her finger at me saying, "He's a devil! Your son is a devil. He pulled this bicycle helmet off my granddaughter's head, broke the strap and nearly strangled her! He's a devil. He is never to come down the street again."

I was stunned and turned to the little girl. "I am so sorry. What happened? Were you playing together?"

She responded, "I wasn't wearing the helmet at the time. He picked it up and threw it." Well, that was quite a different picture. I offered to get an extra helmet that we had.

The grandmother started in again. "He's going to put somebody's eye out. He has a sling-shot. He's a menace."

The little girl said "It's big elastic." Boy, was I glad she was there with the simpler truths.

Despite her granddaughter's variations on the stories, the grand-mother continued to call my son a devil and tell me he was not to come down the street again. I told her that she could restrict him from her yard. "Let me know where you live and I'll tell him. But you cannot restrict him from our neighborhood."

During this harangue, Dan came home. At my prompting, he apol-ogized to the granddaughter about breaking the strap on her helmet, and they walked away.

Later that afternoon, with Matt in the carriage, the three of us walked down the street to the park. On our return we took the cross street where the grandmother lived. She was coming out of the house as we walked by on the other side of the street. She began to yell and gesture wildly, pointing at us and at houses in the vicinity. "He's not welcome here! The So-and-So's don't want him, the So-and-So's don't want him. . . ."

Dan began to cry silently. I want to believe I said something in the moment, but I might not have. I was horrified and completely taken aback.

I know I tried to comfort Dan and felt completely inadequate. I tried to reassure him that she clearly was having a problem—it wasn't him. I called one of the neighbors the grandmother had mentioned in her outburst to see if Dan had been a problem in any way. I didn't think he was a troublemaker or particularly rough in his play with others, but I wanted to check in with another parent whom I knew. The dad told me Dan needed no more correction or talking to than any other kid. No particular problems. He was familiar with the family living next door, and didn't seem surprised by the outburst I described.

Later that weekend, I joined friends in a multiracial family group in which I participated. This group included several interracial couples, and many others who, like me, had adopted children with different racial and ethnic backgrounds than their own. We had a potluck for the adults that gave us an opportunity to talk about our parenting challenges and experiences as multiracial families. I told my story and one of the men in the group really called me out. "Marylou, this is racism. You have to name it! This is what's happening in your neighborhood now. What will they accuse him of when he's a teenager? You have to deal with this."

But deal with it how? I was breathless and scared. I didn't know what to do.

I went to speak to my pastor. I remember feeling comforted in some way, but I am not sure exactly what either of us said.

I came away deciding to write a letter to the grandmother. I tried to be clear but not combative. I took the tack that I had been thinking about what happened, trying to understand it. I concluded that it was unconscious racism. I remember saying that something a blond-haired blue-eyed girl does can be interpreted entirely differently from the same action taken by a brown-skinned boy. I sent the letter to the grandmother and I sent copies to a number of neighbors, including those she had named as "not wanting him here."

With the neighbors' letters, I included another note thanking them for keeping the neighborhood welcoming and safe. No one said a word to me about them. So much for feeling safe and welcomed! I had lived in this neighborhood for over 16 years, long before I adopted my two sons.

This episode was a source of great anguish for me. I was terrified at my own ignorance and ineptitude in supporting my son. I didn't know what else to do. I wondered how many experiences he would have that I would never know about. Had other things already happened? I didn't know how to ask him. Would asking make it worse? I wondered how I should prepare him for racism and prejudice in the world.

That fall I was coming to the conclusion that we needed to move to a town with a stronger school system. It was hard for me—I loved my home. It was close to my work. I had good childcare nearby. I realize in retrospect that this horrible experience in the neighborhood propelled my final decision to move. How I could I be so attached to a place that had been so cruel to my son?  By Easter, my house was sold and we were gone—new town, new challenges.

I thought about this episode many, many times but I didn't realize that I hadn't talked to Dan about it. It was many years later—he was in high school at least—when some conversation we had turned to this. He called the grandmother "the old lady" and told me she had been nice to him. Just the day before, she had given him some very good hot chocolate. Dan's memory is that when she accosted us on the street, I did tell her to stop and that she was out of line. He doesn't remember me comforting him. I had never told him of my letters or the struggles to respond to her outrageous behavior. It opened up whole new wounds from this sad chapter—I was heartbroken at my limitations, my feelings of failure as a parent dealing with unconscious racism for which I was unprepared.

I think often of my friend's demand: "This is racism—you have to name it—you have to deal with it." It seems so obvious, but it is an enormous challenge. I continue to be stunned that a grown woman could be so cruel to a young child. Yet honestly the hurt that haunts me is that my neighbors of 16 years were silent.

There's a saying that silence is complicity, and I guess that's the way I felt at the time—betrayed, let down. Yet that experience of silence fundamentally changed my perspective. When have I been silent, struggling with the right thing to say? I know I am silent at times when I witness racism, cruelty, and injustice. I am not good at a spontaneous response because I need to think about things, ponder. But then I don't know how to get back to it. I've struggled with what I might have done differently to make this an opportunity for opening things up—for discussion and more shared reflection. That's what I hoped for in my letter writing.

And I wonder now, as you read this story, what questions come to your mind? What would you do?

# trading places

## dorothy cresswell

It was August, 1967. I was fourteen, an awkward age, caught between childhood and adulthood. My mother, an inner-city school counselor, had volunteered me to work at a summer camp. The campers and staff all came from a certain neighborhood in Washington, D.C. while I was the only participant from the suburbs of Maryland. The camp had run low on funding so the staff was spending the weekend raising money for the final session.

It was a hot, humid day in Washington, D.C. Since no one wanted to cook, our fundraising meals were a welcome offer. We entered the shop with confidence, simply delivering what they had ordered.

The strung beads hanging down across the store's doorway rattled as we entered. Our hands steadied the full plates of southern-fried chicken, corn, and biscuits for this address. First Porky, then Charlene, and then I stepped in, each balancing large plates laden with food, filling the store with mouthwatering aromas.

"Um-um-um! That smells good!" they greeted Porky and Charlene. There was a welcoming hum of rhythmic music and conversation as we entered.

Then the place went silent. The music was flipped off. Eyes went to the floor. Uncomfortably, I held my heavy plates, wanting to set them down. But I didn't dare move. Something was definitely wrong.

Finally the woman behind the counter demanded, "Why'd you bring her in here? You know we don't allow whites!" I think she spit at me.

Oh, dear God. I was the problem. Please, please, let me disappear.

I was ashamed of my skin color for the first time in my life. The people here were black. The storekeepers and customers were black. The other camp counselors were black. I was as white as the paper plates I held. I was immediately despised and distrusted because of the color of my skin. I couldn't change it. I thought, "But you don't know me. I'm not a bad white person! I'm a good white person! You didn't give me a chance." But I didn't say a word.

My face turned red as a beet, embarrassed not to be black. This white teen-ager do-gooder was a liability to the cause. The hatred coming at me tasted bitter and made my mouth dry. I hardly dared to breathe. My co-counselors were stunned into silence, struggling with conflicting allegiances. Sure, they'd known me a few weeks and let me into their world, but that was out in the countryside of Maryland where they were strangers in a strange land. In my land! Now I was in their neighborhood, and I didn't fit in here. Finally Charlene said, "You'd better leave. We'll deliver these."

Trembling, not sure what I had done wrong, but feeling very wrong, and much too visible in my out-of-place-ness, I left as quickly as I could. It was all I could do to return to the van. I couldn't say a word. I had just been blatantly treated the way they had been blatantly and less-blatantly treated for their whole lives. That was their haven and I was not welcome.

My parents had moved up from Mississippi in the early 1950s because they were so disgusted with the prejudices and narrow-mindedness of the Deep South. They prided themselves in working for social justice above the Mason-Dixon line. They had refused membership in a local country club when they learned that blacks and Jews were not accepted. I had been raised on discussions of civil rights and equality. I had tearfully listened to Martin Luther King, Jr.'s "I Have A Dream" speech when I was ten years old, standing in the crowd on the Mall between the White House and the Washington Monument. I had already taken the non-violence trainings offered in church basements when Martin Luther King, Jr. was in the D.C. area.

I thought I knew all about racism. I knew things were unfair. I had seen "Whites Only" signs in Mississippi on restaurants, gas station bathrooms, and water fountains. I knew how very wrong that was. But I only knew as an observer. I knew the principles of inequity. I knew my home was nicer than my campers' homes. As one little boy said to me, "I bet you even have a refrigerator!" I certainly did, and had never realized that some families a few miles inside of the D.C. line might not have one.

But I did not know until that very afternoon what it was like to walk inside skin where one was judged and cast out before one even said a word. In my heart of hearts, I knew I could not complain to anyone about how I had been treated for five miserable minutes in that store. This was how they had been treated for the entire history of our country. Generation to generation, their skin color had determined where they could go and how they were treated.

I had only been treated as they had been treated. Ow, ow, ow, ow, ouch. The hurting was so deep, and not located in any single place. I curled up in that van and rubbed and rubbed my arms and legs, but could not wipe away the feeling of dirtiness and pain. There was no bandage or bath that could appease the injury to my soul. I was never angry at what happened that day. I was only immensely embarrassed by my whiteness, by being a member of the oppressive culture.

The following year, in April of 1968, Martin Luther King, Jr. was assassinated. Riots broke out in the city. In my safe brick home in Montgomery County, I got a phone call. My camp counselor friend Porky had been shot and killed by the police.

"What? What happened?" I begged to understand.

"He was among the looters. He was holding a man's tailored shirt and he ran when the police came. They shot him in the back."

Porky was handsome, funny, warm-hearted, and great with the children. I'd had a crush on him and his big grin and sparkling eyes! Those white-skinned police had taken down a great kid. They never gave him a chance.

"He was in the wrong place at the wrong time," the caller explained.

President Johnson signed the Civil Rights Act of 1969 one week later. Forty years have passed. I'd like to think that the situation is significantly different. But at a friend's birthday party this very year, I met two strong black women, about my age, who worked with the public school.

One declared, "My brown babies don't get treated the same as the white kids at school."

Oh, how I wanted to argue that that wasn't true, being a teacher myself. But I decided to listen. I asked questions and tried to understand.

"They get slotted into Special Education programs, and kept there with a label, stuck forever in that less-able-than category."

Hmm.

The other woman gave an example of a student of color, her niece, who had received special education while she needed it but was no longer on an Individual Education Plan. Now she was getting strong grades in the regular education program and had been accepted to a college.

"The system is working for her," she stated.

So there is some hope. At the same time, there are still significant pockets all over this country, north and south, where the schools and school resources are dramatically less from town to town and county to county, particularly where the populations are mostly of people of color; where there may or may not be a refrigerator in the home; or where one may or may not get shot in the back before one graduates from high school.

We are not living the dream yet.

# don't look it up

## gretchen curry

I was born in Portland, Connecticut, a town tucked in a bend of the Connecticut River, twenty miles south of Hartford, the state capital. I lived across the parking lot from my dad's church in a large white house that was owned by the parish. I learned to ride my bike on the roads of the graveyard behind my house. Weekends were spent rollerblading with neighborhood friends and roasting s'mores over the grill in the backyard. I even had a lemonade stand with my sister and best friend from across the street. From kindergarten on, I remember there was a housing development on my bus route down by the boat yard. All the African American and Hispanic kids got off the bus at that stop. It took me years to figure out why.

When I was nine, I moved to Bloomfield, Connecticut with my family. Bloomfield is a town right outside of Hartford, full of African-American and West-Indian families anxious to escape the inner-city schools and the violence that haunts the capital's streets. I was in the fourth grade and the only white person in my class with the exception of my teacher, Mr. Schwager. I was very nervous at first in this new school, but my anxiety quickly faded as Mr. Schwager helped me feel as comfortable as possible in my new setting. He kept a close eye on me those first few weeks. Only now do I realize the sympathy he had for me and how I benefited from his special attention.

Recess served as a time of both entrapment and escape. I confidently showed off my four-square skills (a blacktop game where four kids bounce around a ball within four painted squares trying to get each other "out" by bouncing the ball in their own square or out of bounds) and gained some credibility on the playground, but could never master the complexity of double-dutch. Just as I was starting to feel comfortable, one event brought me back to the reality that I really was different in this new community.

It was during the paired reading portion of our honors language arts class. My friend Tameshia and I were sitting on a carpet in the back corner. We were taking turns reading aloud to each other from a book set in the south in the 1940s. Our parents had signed a permission slip in order for us to read this particular story in class because of the racial content that it presented.

I had just finished reading my section. Tameshia began hers and then skipped right over one of the words in the paragraph without stopping. I looked up at her and sounded out the word, thinking she was having trouble doing so. "The word is 'nigger'," I offered. Tears welled up in her eyes. "It's 'nigger'," I repeated, trying to help. Tameshia kept her eyes glued to the ground, fighting back tears, then stood up and left the room.

Emily and Amena, my Filipino and Afghani friends, were sitting just a few feet away. I overheard them discussing the same word with curiosity. They began to look through the dictionary. Distraught and upset, I turned towards them.

"Don't look it up," I said. They looked up at me, catching my strong tone. "Just don't."

Two years later, I moved to West Hartford where I attended middle and high school in more fully integrated schools. Because of this experience, I decided to take a year after high school to do something for myself that a college education could not offer. I joined City Year, a division of AmeriCorps that brings young people of all backgrounds together for ten months of community service in U.S. cities. Two months out of high school, I packed up all my things and moved to San Antonio, Texas.

I didn't have much to live on. I moved into a shabby but comfortable house with three other Corps members on the east side of the city. San Antonio is one of the most segregated cities in America, and I stood out in my new neighborhood like a sore thumb. "What are you gringos doing over here?" soon became a familiar question on my travels to work each day.

One Sunday afternoon, I was waiting at my usual bus stop to go downtown. The handicap alcove offered a little more distance between me and the honks and whistles from passing cars. My attention shifted when I saw a police car drive towards me. He stopped at the red light directly across from me and got on his intercom so that I and any passerby could hear.

"Are you OK?" he asked.

I looked at him strangely. "Yes."

"What are you doing?"

"I'm waiting for the bus." I pointed to the bus sign above me.

"OK," he said, in a voice that was far from convinced. "Have a good day."

I was bothered and angry. It was as if I was nine years old again; the white authority figure protecting me from an environment that he believed I did not fit into.

Near the end of my volunteer year, I was once again at the bus stop but on a weekday in my work uniform. Again a police car approached, only this time the cop was black.

"Where are you going?"

"To work," I said, in no way trying to hide the frustration in my voice.

"Where do you work?"

"At Miller Academy, up the street."

He was on his phone and seemed distracted, but wouldn't let up until he was reassured that I really did have somewhere to be.

"OK. Have a nice day."

"Yeah, you too," I replied, thinking, "I will never get used to this."

Yes, I was a white girl on the eastside. Yes, I was going to use the bus. And no, I was not there to buy drugs. My house was in fact just up the street. Yes, this was my home.

# freddy's secret

## susan daniels

My grandfather was from the South. He was born in Hernando, Mississippi and lived out most of his days in Memphis, Tennessee. He had been a successful businessman and in his retirement, he grew peaches. He had two orchards that bordered his home and he hired three black men to work with him in the orchards. Freddy was my favorite. He was loyal to my grandfather, and subsequently to the Yankee grandchildren that visited from New England every summer. Freddy called me "Miz Susan." My brothers were "Mr. Tom" and "Mr. Pete" and my Dad was "Mr. Bill." Only my grandfather held the title, "Mr. Daniels."

My grandfather smoked cigars. All the time! Even when they weren't lit, he would chew the stubs around in his mouth, especially when he was thinking over a response to a particularly tricky question. When he died, we put a cigar in his shirt pocket. It stuck out a little so that everyone who passed by the open casket could see and smile and remember. Freddy chewed tobacco from a pouch.

Freddy was old. Nobody knew his exact age, but there was a lot of speculation and jokes about it. The fact was, though, that no matter how old Freddy was, my grandfather was older than that, and Freddy had a lot of respect for my old, still hard-working grandfather. He also had respect for my grandfather having money, having land, and for growing such big beautiful fruit on that land. You often found my grandfather out in the orchard during the day, checking on the crops, picking some pole beans for my grandmother to cook up for supper, and sometimes taking a rest in an old metal folding chair, having a smoke.

Freddy was always happy to see me each summer, but it was a practiced kind of happy, the kind of smiling and fussing you make over "Miz Susan, Mr. Daniels' granddaughter." I noticed Freddy had a more serious side, especially during his early morning meetings with my grandfather in the driveway. After getting the instructions for the day's work, Freddy became the boss, heading out into the orchard, his territory, to complete that day's tasks. I looked forward to the times when I could walk down that driveway with Freddy, buckets in hand, and head out with him to the orchard, where I could at least go through the motions of being the same as him. It was the early 1970s, the women's movement was in full swing, and bussing in Memphis had just started. I wanted to get it right.

My opportunity came sooner than I expected. My family and I moved from Massachusetts to Memphis. I was thirteen and trying desperately to adjust to the heat, the high school girls and their parents who would inquire from the front seat of the carpool, "You're not from here, are you?"

Freddy had been a constant for me since childhood and I felt good about working during the summers alongside him in the orchard, dressing in denim overalls like him, and trying out different ways to make my bandana look stylish. From Freddy, I learned the art of keeping sweat out of my eyes and peach fuzz off my arms and the importance of drinking lots of water and taking regular breaks in the Cold House, a big freezer-type hut used for storage. Freddy wasn't just old, he was wise: wise about life in and out of the orchard.

One day during our Cold House break, Freddy asked me if I knew anything about tobacco, and wondered if I could check a book out of the library for him addressing the subject. I was thrilled to do this favor for him and the next day during our break, I proudly produced a worn, hardbound library book entitled *Tobacco, Its History and Uses.* Freddy pulled up alongside me in one of the metal folding chairs and asked me to read it to him. I love to read out loud and I took this request as another opportunity to be helpful, to be useful. He listened carefully as I read the first three paragraphs about the Europeans coming to America and John Rolfe and the Virginia plantations. I noticed how hard he was concentrating on the words, his head turned away from the book itself, his eyes half-shut. Every now and then he'd shake his head and ask me to skip a few pages and read something else, maybe go to another chapter. I ended up reading every chapter title in the table of contents before Freddy finally gave up.

The book I had checked out of the library was wrong; it was not the book he needed. It seemed that my grandfather had given him a little plot of land in back of the south orchard to use as he wished. Freddy's dream was to grow tobacco in that plot so that he could roll and smoke his own cigars like my grandfather. He wanted a book about how to grow tobacco, not the history of tobacco, and he needed me to read him the instructions because he couldn't read. I offered to get him another book, but he said that was OK, he didn't really need it. He never brought it up again and this became a secret between Freddy and me forever. His cigar dream, my reading to him in the Cold House, my getting it all wrong.

# casualty

## ivy tillman

My mother died when I was six years old, my younger brother was four, and my baby sister was two. I can't say that we were a wildly happy family, but we were happy enough. I attended a Seventh-Day Adventist church, and I had two working parents who were, to all appearance, well-respected in the church and the community. At the time of the accident, we had a large extended family: the maternal side lived in the city and the paternal side lived in the rural outskirts of that city. Oh yes, we all lived in Mecklenburg County, North Carolina, and the year was 1958.

I don't know the particulars of the accident, really. My father, while we still spoke to one other, would not talk about it to me. All I know is that my mother was in a car accident, and that she was in the city's hospital. I remember sitting in a car outside the hospital for a very long time. I have a vague memory of the wake, some rather vivid memories of the funeral—my whole school was there. I think I remember what my mother was wearing, and I remember "Nearer, My God, to Thee" was sung—and then, my mother was gone, forever.

So, what does this have to do with racism, you might ask? It was

49

thirty years before I found out the truth, although the effects on relationships within my family were felt long before.

When I was seventeen and a new high-school graduate, I moved into an apartment with my father for the summer between high school and college. While snooping through my father's papers—goodness, I hope that's a normal teenage activity!—I found my mother's death certificate. My father had told us that our mother had died from double pneumonia. The death certificate did list this as the primary cause of death, but the secondary cause was phlebothrombosis—a blood clot—in the lungs precipitated by an attempted illegal abortion. There was no mention of an accident, or any trauma caused by an accident. Just the abortion.

When confronted, my father's only response was that I should not have been looking through his things. He did not say, "That piece of paper lies."

This was the beginning of a strain in our relationship that lasts to this day. I believed—and held—my father responsible for my mother's death for a very long time. They were married, and she would not have attempted an abortion except with his consent or at his command. Or so I believed. From then on, I found and wore a button that displayed a coat hanger with the "prohibited" red circle and slash that read "Never another illegal abortion."

I lost touch with most of my family after ending my first foray into higher education, but as years went by and I settled into adulthood, some ties with my relatives on my mother's side were re-established. Some happened because I reached out. In other cases, family members reached out to me.

I used to talk to one of my uncles—the first of my uncles to whom I came out—on the phone two or three times a year. One day, after I had been talking about my mother's death, and badmouthing my dad for causing it, my uncle said something that stopped me cold. He said "Denise, your mother did not try to have an abortion. I visited her in the hospital, and she told me that she knew she was dying, that the person who had hit her car was a white woman, and that woman was at fault in the accident. She told me that 'they' were not going to charge a white woman with seriously injuring a Negro woman, even a pregnant one. So, when she died, the death certificate didn't record the accident, but did record the termination of a pregnancy. And your father—a Negro man in the South in 1958—knew better than to protest. But Denise, he has had to live with that and with your anger all these years. It was racism that killed your mother—the racism that put her in a substandard hospital that did not offer to Negros the same level of care that would have been offered to a white, the racism that did not pursue and prosecute a white for the death of a Negro. It was the racist South, Denise, which your father felt he couldn't fight. I don't know why he couldn't say this to you. Maybe he would rather you think him cruel than weak. I don't know."

My mother's death split up our family. After she died, my two siblings and I lived with my maternal grandmother in an urban industrial city in the North. After five years, my father briefly reclaimed us. Then he left us with his mother in rural Mecklenberg County. The rest of our childhood was shaken and broken. To be truthful, my father's parenting skills were shaken and broken, too—he was only 27 when his wife, his family anchor, was lost.

Since that conversation with my uncle, I have let my father off the hook for the death of my mother. And while our relationship is still broken, I don't think him weak for not fighting the institution of racism—in the hospital, county, and city. It was, and still is, a tough battle for one person.

# racism in my family

## alia starkweather

I grew up in White Plains, New York, a small city (then) 40 miles north
of New York City. My grandmother and grandfather lived across town,
about three miles away. They had what we called a "colored" woman
who cleaned house for my grandmother. When I was 12, we moved into
my grandmother's house because she was quite sick. The "colored
woman" was named Cora. She had a last name, Tolliver, but she was
always called Cora. I had been taught to call my mother's friends "Mrs.
French," "Mrs. Turner," but Cora, who had a grown son, was "Cora."

My family was upper middle-class. Even the women had had some
college education for several generations. We were Protestant, sometimes
Methodist, sometimes Presbyterian, and sometimes Congregational,
depending, I think, on whether my mother liked the minister. My
parents did not go to church regularly but sent my brother and me to
Sunday school.

My grandparents belonged to the NAACP, the National Association
for the Advancement of Colored People. We always used the word
"Negro" if we did not say colored, and never the "nigger" word. It was
never spoken in my home, except once when my father told me that in

53

the rhyme "eeny, meeny, miny, mo, catch a bunny by the toe," some people, in some places, used "nigger" instead of "bunny." I can still see the deep frown on my mother's face when my father spoke the terrible word.

And yet, we, the educated, unprejudiced family, called Cora "Cora," instead of Mrs. Tolliver. She never sat down to eat with us. She called my mother "Mrs. Goreth," and my grandmother, "Mrs. Palmer."

When I was three years old, I was very sick with scarlet fever. This is a complication of streptococcus that is now easily curable with antibiotics, but back then, there was no cure, just quarantining the house and keeping the patient isolated from everyone except the mother or nurse. I asked for Cora because she was the person who was able to love me better than anyone else.

This is the insidiousness of racism. It is almost invisible, especially when all the adults collude—even unconsciously—in presenting the same perspective in the same way. I grew up believing my family had no prejudice, but it is easy to see that we did, and it was not too subtle if one knew how to look for it.

I still regret that as I grew older and overwhelmed with family needs, I did not make the effort to keep up with Cora, who died of complications from diabetes when I was 25 or so. She was a lovely, wonderful person, but to us she was mostly "the maid."

# growing up

## robert stover

I spent part of my childhood living in Santa Barbara, California and I retain two memories from that part of my life that pertain to prejudice and racism.

We moved to Santa Barbara in January of 1956 because my father took a job as a bacteriologist at the Santa Barbara County Hospital. My parents rented a modest house that had, at least for a kid, a lot of character and many charms. It was on Grand Avenue. Grand Avenue ascends a steep hill opposite the Pacific coast and overlooks the city.

Perhaps this is the same mountain that John C. Fremont tumbled down, with his mules and troopers, when they surprised and defeated the Spanish garrison to claim Santa Barbara for the U.S.A. At any rate, we had a great view of the city and the ocean.

The house was perched high above the road with a high stone wall rising five or six feet from the edge of the sidewalk to the terrace that was our narrow front yard. At the back of this yard, wide stone steps rose up about four more feet to the next terrace upon which was a stone patio and the first floor of our house.

My mother, then about twenty-seven or eight, took pleasure in cele-brating the Spanish heritage of Santa Barbara. For what we would now probably call a cheap play date, she took us kids to romp around on the well-groomed grounds of Santa Barbara's Spanish mission. This mission was featured in the New York Times "Travel" section a few years ago, and it's still a must-see attraction for visitors to Santa Barbara. Once, my mother costumed me up as a Spanish caballero and my sister Sarah and our friend Mousy as Spanish senoras and we all walked in a parade. There is a photograph somewhere verifying this memory.

Mousy is the one neighborhood pal I still remember from that era. She's more or less Sarah's age, about three years younger than me. Her parents are Swiss and she spoke English fluently but with an accent. The other kids in the neighborhood were all, like my family, white Americans.

I attended a public elementary school and, overwhelmingly, the kids in the school were also white Americans. One year there were excep-tions. It was probably second grade. In the class were two Spanish-speaking students with skin just slightly darker than our own. I imagine that they were Mexicans and that they were siblings. Their English was serviceable but not as good as Mousy's. As I recall, their dress and manners were pretty much the same as those of the rest of us in the class.

Nonetheless, our teacher treated them harshly right from the get-go. On the first day of class, she found fault with their school supplies and on every following day, something about them was scornfully criticized. The two students sat quietly through this abuse without protesting. They blushed with expressions of pain and shame. They were second graders. I don't know how or whether they endured this treatment for a whole school year. My memory isn't clear on this, but it's possible that they were driven off and pulled out of our school.

I don't remember anything else about that teacher except that she was, like all teachers in those days, an old lady—probably in her mid-twenties.

I recall a second incident from those days in Santa Barbara that concerned race and prejudice. It involved my mother but she doesn't remember it.

My parents drove us north of Santa Barbara to an almost tropical nature preserve. I recall it as just a day trip but my mother thinks it might have been the day we drove away from Santa Barbara when we moved to Rockford, Illinois.

As my sister and I played on the wide and well-maintained footpaths and footbridges in the preserve, a man with very black, very African skin walked by us. We must have reacted very obviously and very giddily in our astonishment at the color of his skin because my mother immediately collared us and sat us down. With an adamancy that was not typical of her in those days, she told us that not only was our behavior unseemly and no doubt an embarrassment to the gentleman who had walked by us but that other than the obvious difference in skin color, he was in every essential way exactly like us and that under no circumstances were we ever to make fun of or mistreat another person because they have a skin color different from our own.

My mother doesn't remember this incident but I have thought of it many times in my adult life. I've wondered how she came to hold this point of view; what does it say about her own upbringing; what does it say about the attitudes prevalent in the small farm towns in northern Nebraska where she was raised in the thirties and forties.

I asked my mother these questions and a more complicated picture emerged. There were no African Americans in the small town in which she grew up. A Lebanese-American merchant and his family did live in the town. Their darker skin and different ethnic heritage were noted but, as far as my mother could recall, the community accepted this family. My mother and one of the merchant's daughters went to school together.

A white American living in northern Nebraska in the thirties and forties was much more likely to encounter Native Americans than African Americans. Native Americans apparently were targets of ethnic hostility from at least some members of the white community.

According to my mother's recollection, this hostility was commonly justified or rationalized or expressed in terms of criticisms of differing lifestyles and personal hygiene habits.

My mother's own commitment to racial tolerance seems to have come from her mother. My grandmother seems to have believed that a good and decent person, a person who has been well brought-up, doesn't engage in racism. However, my mother does recall one conversation long ago when my grandmother opined that white and black persons probably shouldn't go to the same beaches since this might lead to romantic attractions among them that, in her opinion, would probably be unwise.

My mother recalls that, following her high school graduation, she took the train to central Florida where she spent the summer working for one of her uncles. This was probably the summer of 1946. In Florida she did witness racism toward African Americans. Her uncle was a doctor in general practice and received patients at a home office. She doesn't believe that this uncle was a racist but white American patients entered through the front door into a waiting room and African-Americans patients were seen on the back porch.

Upon her return to Nebraska she began college at the University of Nebraska at Lincoln. In her first year there she shared a gym locker with an African-American woman. Despite the fact that this was her first real personal contact with an African American apparently neither of them regarded this experience as especially remarkable.

Like my mother, I have lived my own life in rural, suburban and exurban America primarily in the company of other white Americans. With very few exceptions, the white Americans I have spent my life with have not regarded themselves to be racists; on the contrary, they have considered themselves to be antagonistic to racism. So I believe that the family attitudes on racism that I experienced can't be so very different from those of millions other white Americans.

I realize that the racism I refer to herein is conscious and overt racism. I realize also that there are less conscious and less overt forms of racism. I realize that there is racism built into our system and institutions. But, still I believe there is something to be learned by contemplating that, alongside the explicit racism and the paroxysms of violent racism that some people in our country have suffered there, have also been the attitudes toward race that I and many others were taught.

# reflections from a catholic childhood

## joanne sunshower

Rachel Farmer was the first African-American person I ever knew. In 1954, my fifth brother was born, and my father decided it was time to hire a helper for my mother. Rachel was referred to us by the pastor of a neighboring church. She was good natured and diligent, helping our family through the most difficult years of multiple toddlers growing into elementary school. She started going to church with us, eventually took catechism lessons, and joined the Catholic Church. Rachel and my mother became very close. Even after she moved on to another family, they still kept in touch. Their bond was a shared faith and an understanding of the role of love and forgiveness in lessening life's suffering.

For the most part, I liked Rachel and was happy playing my part as the eldest, helping her as I would my mother. We would tell jokes or sing songs while working. Sometimes I was resentful—of having to do my share of the chores, of my mother not being as available for me as much as I wanted, of having someone besides my mother telling me what to do. At those times, Rachel would tell me earnestly how lucky I was to have such a large and loving family, and remind me that the tasks she asked of me were what my mother wanted me to do.

I'm sure that wasn't always the end of it. Sometimes I just needed to let my feelings out before I could settle back into what I knew were my responsibilities. Somehow Rachel knew that, and after our talk would go on about her work, and leave me to do mine in my own time. As I grew older, I asked her about her life outside work. I found out she had children older than me, that she liked to dance, and we became as friendly as a child and adult can be. I found myself helping her when I didn't have to, and making her little "I love you" cards.

This early personal experience set the stage for my understanding of the civil rights movement. My high school in Kansas City, St. Teresa's Academy, was not well-integrated but there were Asian, African, and Latino Americans among the teachers and students. Most of our families were working and professional middle class. News and discussion of the civil rights movement was prominent in our social science classes. Several of our teachers, Sisters of St. Joseph, went on the walk from Selma to Montgomery. This context and the community of my faith led me straight into taking responsibility and becoming a public advocate.

A few of us followed the lead of one of our teachers to help create a High School Interracial Council. We didn't change the world, but we did change our lives simply by getting together with those from other schools to talk about the civil rights movement, the racial division of neighborhoods in Kansas City, and holding social events where we had a chance to have fun together. Volleyball tournaments added to our experience with diversity as a norm. The teams from different parts of town showed more or less diversity than ours but all were similar in being seriously competitive, emotional about wins and losses, and disciplined with good sportsmanship.

For me, there was one wrinkle to being on the Interracial Council. To account for the time I spent on this activity, I told my father I was attending French Club because he was vehement about crossing racial lines in town, and about political troublemakers. In the midst of watching a news story about people from the North joining the civil rights work in the South, he said if any of us ever got mixed up in something like that, we had better be ready to live on our own.

With a mixture of his own natural good humor and prejudice he inherited from his parents, my father could rail against different ethnic groups in general but was genuine with anyone he knew personally. This was true of Rachel, and of Albert, an orderly from the hospital whose wife had stabbed him in a rage. My father invited him to stay with us while he sorted things out. This was also true of my father's feelings about the commanding officer at the Army recruiting station where he worked as an examining physician, a man whom my father admired and praised for his competence, and occasionally invited home for dinner.

The west side of Kansas City was the Latino district, Spanish-speaking as we said back then. Through an introduction by a visiting missionary priest, I met the Spanish Sisters of Mercy, and spent many weekends working in their nursing home. The bus ride there took me into neighborhoods of poverty that frightened me—gray houses losing their paint, and children looking not-well-cared-for. The disabilities from age and disease of some of the residents in the nursing home also frightened me. But the sisters cared for them with cheerfulness and sincerity. Working beside them, I learned to share their spirit.

It was a spirit lit early, blowing on the coals of morning prayer, reinforced with kindness, laughter, pride in work, and periods of prayer throughout the day.

Occasionally I was asked to go with two of them, visiting families with food and medicine, and helped by playing with the children while the nurses attended to the parents and grandparents. And so I learned a little Spanish, and how God's love and joyful companions can overcome fear of the unfamiliar, sickness, and poverty.

There are other experiences as well—of the ghetto highrise in Kansas City, of Roxbury, Massachusetts, of wartime Nicaragua. I learned to navigate each one under the wings of courageous, spiritually grounded women and men. A diversity of ethnicities, of languages, of ages, of personalities, ministries and gifts—but all with the same spirit.

transformations

# a world of trouble

## hari stephen kumar

"Are you married to that man?"

The question came flying out to Alexis from the driver's window of a minivan that had pulled up next to our rental car. I had noticed the minivan earlier, cruising slowly up the street behind us as we walked to our car, hand in hand, pleasantly chatting about plans for that summer evening in St. Louis. I opened the passenger door of our rental car for my wife as the van drew up alongside, and I headed to the back of the car to heft my laptop bag into the trunk. I was in St. Louis on business, so at the end of the work day I was still in smart business attire and I was looking forward to relaxing over dinner. Hearing my wife talking with the stranger in the van, I walked up to join the conversation.

When my wife replied that we were indeed married, and at the point that I walked up to stand beside Alexis, the middle-aged white woman driving the minivan looked shocked. Ignoring me completely, she asked Alexis, "But, isn't he from Pakistan or some place like that?"

Alexis said, "No, he's from India actually."

The woman dismissively replied, "It's the same thing..." and then leaned out to caution Alexis, "you're in for a world of trouble!"

Alexis, still smiling, still sweet, asked, "Why?"

And the woman, still ignoring me completely, said, "Well, they oppress women where he comes from!"

*Now there's a good question—where DO I come from? Ever since I can remember, I have been a foreigner. I was born in India but I grew up in Yemen, in the Middle East, from the ages of seven through sixteen. Even there, my shade of South Indian brown was darker than the sandy complexion of my Yemeni friends, who promptly came up with creative insults based on my darkness. It did not help that I was a devout Hindu Brahmin boy growing up in a very orthodox Islamic country.*

*When I came to America for graduate school in the late 1990s, I also went through a profoundly gut-wrenching spiritual transformation during which I became a Christian in a way that caused profound grief for my parents and family back in India. For them, Christianity represented an historically racist attack on their cultural identities, and my Christianity was (and remains) a betrayal too deep for words. However, as a Christian here in America, especially here in New England, I have experienced an almost obsessive tolerance from others that has helped me explore my own identity with very few personal racist attacks.*

*Sometimes I wonder if one of the reasons I have encountered so few elements of racism directed at me, personally, in America is because I exhibit a white way of living, especially in speaking an English that is white American. I grew up learning English as my first language, a necessary skill given my family's global wanderings, and in Yemen I studied in a school that had English teachers from America, Great Britain, and Australia. I grew up with a stronger command of grammar and diction than most Americans. Now, after more than a decade of living in Massachusetts, when I hear someone compliment me on my English, I reply, "Thank you, and yours is pretty good too!"*

*But that didn't matter to the woman who accosted my wife, did it? I hadn't had a chance to speak but I was well dressed and for all she knew, I could be from New Jersey! Yet the color of my skin marks me more than my clothes....*

The woman continued to Alexis, "You know what will happen if you go to his country, don't you? His culture oppresses women and treats them as sex objects! He will oppress you and never let you come back!"

Alexis sweetly replied, "Well, actually we are going to visit his family this winter, and I am looking forward to it!"

The stunned woman whispered, "Oh, you are in for such a world of trouble!"

*Alexis and I met in January 2005, immediately fell into the kind of love that I never believed in until I met her, and we were married in June that year. My parents were vehemently opposed to the wedding because Alexis is a white American woman. They told me that white American women were all like the ones they saw on TV or heard about from their friends' sons—oversexed and unfaithful and selfishly dominant. Life would become hell for me.*

*They eventually came around to the idea, and tried to make it to our Christian wedding even though my father said he "would be humiliated by them." I can only imagine who or what he meant by "them." As it turned out, they did not make it in time due to US visa complications. So they never met or spoke with Alexis until shortly after our wedding. And then they fell in love with her. They still resent me for betraying them, but they love Alexis.*

*We went to visit my family in the winter of 2006. We traveled first to the United Kingdom where my sister and her husband (an orthodox Indian Brahmin surgeon, chosen by my family) lived with their son. We then traveled to Egypt where we spent two weeks with my parents, and the four of us then went to India to visit the rest of the extended clan.*

*Alexis wore Indian dress for most of the trip, wowing my mother, and generally being the sweet person she always is. In India, my relatives commented on how Alexis was more observant of traditionally conservative Indian values and dress style than my young cousins who thrived on the latest Hollywood fashions.*

The evening sun glittered off a stained-glass cross that swung on a necklace under the lady's chin. I asked her: "Excuse me, ma'am, I see that you are wearing a cross. Are you a Christian?"

Maybe it was my flawless American accent, or maybe it was my identification of her religion—without revealing my own Christianity—that got her attention, but she replied, "Yes. Why?"

I said, "Well, ma'am, maybe you should read your Bible some more to really understand what God has to say about oppression."

Puzzled, she responded, "I don't know what you mean...."

I don't know exactly why I chose this particular thread, but I plunged on. "Before you accuse my people of oppressing women, you would do well to listen to teenage women right here in your own neighborhood to see how your own culture reduces them to sex objects."

Stunned, the woman exclaimed, "Well! I...I don't know what...I have never been treated as a sex object!"

*Long before I met Alexis, I remember dating a young white woman from South Carolina whose white, middle-aged, middle-class, single mother frequently complained to me about "those lazy blacks who are always saying they are so tired!" She worked long hours as a nurse at a hospital in Charleston, and every evening she had fresh stories about her black colleagues, stories that only got worse as she began drinking her fatigue away over the course of the night.*

*I remember watching TV with the mother one lazy summer evening in Charleston as the news reported an armed robbery at a local convenience store. I remember the mother saying, "Oh just watch now. They're gonna show the suspect and it'll be one of them!" And I remember both mother and daughter crowing in delight when the video clip of the arrested criminal revealed him to, indeed, be "one of them."*

*I remember wondering why the mother felt comfortable sharing her racism against black people with me, the brown guy dating her equally racist daughter at the turn of the new millennium.*

I should have said something snappy along the lines of "Yes, I can see why," but I was beginning to feel foolish, so I simply left it at "Well ma'am, just read your Bible to see what God really has to say about oppression."

The lady shook her head at me, looked at Alexis, and as the minivan started rolling away she said, one last time, "Just be careful, you are in for a world of trouble! They oppress women where he comes from!"

*During our visit to Egypt to see my parents a couple of years ago, I remember opening the passenger doors to my dad's car so that my mother and my wife could get in. I have always enjoyed opening doors for women—I am not a chauvinist, I just like being gentlemanly, even if such a notion is old-fashioned these days.*

*My dad got angry and yelled at me in the car. He said that opening doors for women would be considered effeminate in Egypt and in India, and that I should be more manly.*

*This confused me because my father and I had never really had a discussion about manhood before. It seemed to me, informed by my faith in a God who sacrificed his metaphoric masculinity for his metaphorical bride, that manhood needed to be less about domination and more about service, less about demanding an obedient respect and more about earning a trusted respect. It seemed to me that such a notion of manhood took intensely more work and risk than an oppressive manhood that was all but guaranteed.*

*Opening car doors, and doors in general, are to me a symbolic way of opening doors for women in general—not that my wife cannot open doors on her own but rather that I am voluntarily choosing to honor and respect my wife by putting her before me.*

A day later I came out to see a note under the wiper of my rental car- a note from the lady in the minivan. It was a photocopied sheet of various Bible verses on salvation, with a handwritten scrawl that read: "I am sorry for being so rude yesterday."

Alexis and I were bemused but I was a little bit shaken, too. Here was a woman who assumed so many different things about me, without giving me a chance to perform my "white Christian American" persona for her. My brown appearance carried with it a whole host of commentaries on race and feminist ideologies. And, even though I defended "my people"—whoever they are—my own people think I am somewhat of a wimp for not being more oppressively manly toward my white American wife who, after all, is just "one of them."

I pinned the note on the door outside my office, along with other paraphernalia collected from my travels, and thought nothing more of it. A couple of months later, a coworker named Doug walked by, stopped, and read the note. Upon hearing the back story, Doug laughed and said, "Yeah, I saw you oppressing your wife the other day by holding your car door open for her. How dare you?! You should make her walk ten steps behind you!"

*I think moving beyond racism in America is going to take a counter-cultural performance of race and gender that is not overtly scripted or reasoned or explained, but rather is performed subconsciously in everyday moments.*

*In an election year when Senator Hillary Clinton can tap into the latent unspoken racism of white middle-aged American women while claiming to open doors for women, I think what encourages me most are people like Doug. He had observed us—an interracial couple—in an everyday moment as we enacted our identities in a loving way that said something against unspoken and unchallenged narratives of race and gender. Unlike the woman in the minivan, Doug was someone watching at the right window at the right time.*

# on emotional racism

## heather powers albanesi

I recently experienced what I considered a magnified moment, one that offered me an opportunity to revisit my understanding of the many levels at which racism functions.

For me, it was a moment of intensely heightened stress, and I believe those emotions are relevant to this story.

Two days before my magnified moment, I found out that an MRI (magnetic resonance imaging) had found a tumor—described as enormous for its location—inside my mother's spinal column, wrapped around her spinal cord at the C2 vertebrae. It would have to be removed, and she needed surgery to take place as soon as possible.

Needless to say, the family was in shock and terrified, my mother no less than anyone else.

Two days later, the moment happened. My mother called to say that they had just scheduled the surgery—considered brain surgery due to the tumor's location—for that week. My mother followed that information with the statement that all she knew about her surgeon was that she is a black woman.

My emotional reaction to that news was not inspiring, certainly not my most enlightened moment. While I didn't verbalize these feelings to my mother, my very first emotion was "Yikes!" My first thoughts were, "Is this surgeon really the best? Is this the most talented brain surgeon available?"

Since then, I have given considerable thought as to why I had that kind of reaction. I have always thought of myself as particularly aware of the dynamics of racism and the insidiousness of racial stereotypes. How could I have even momentarily felt that?

Some of my earliest memories of childhood are of my parents' active engagement in anti-racism work. In addition, I was well aware of how different our home was from others. I remember as a little kid, my cousins visiting and making racist jokes and being shocked that anyone would say things like that.

While perhaps a bit overboard in political correctness, my sister and I were not allowed to pretend to be American Indians or even witches— no flying around the house on a broom for us. The extremely liberal, yet very white, small college town I grew up in reinforced this heightened (although uneasy) awareness of racial oppression and unfair stereotypes. In first grade, after the class was assigned to different reading groups, the teacher told us that each group was expected to come up with a name for their group. While my group choose to be the Bunnies, another group decided they would be called the Chiefs. When the teacher asked why they wanted that name, they said it was after a football team. The teacher announced that the name was unacceptable due to its racist connotations, and they would have to come up with a different name. In the insular world I grew up in, to be caught—even inadvertently—saying something racist was shameful, a gauge of your backwardness and ignorance. Needless to say, the issue of racism was always emotionally loaded.

My educational trajectory led me from one uber-liberal institution to another. From Wesleyan University (a small college in Connecticut overtly committed to diversity) for undergraduate school to Berkeley (a university famous for its liberal activism) for graduate school. While thankfully more racially diverse than the town I grew up in, both institutions were fairly uniform in political diversity, particularly so in the departments and circles in which I moved.

Consistent with my experience growing up, I lived and breathed (and spouted) political correctness. Yet being able to smoothly negotiate the ever-changing language of political correctness was emotionally tied to moving in the world with a sophisticated, cultured, and educated identity. In this world, one's moral commitment, walking the walk, to issues of social justice and inclusion was always suspect, impossible to scrutinize directly, and ultimately secondary to talking the talk.

If anything, this pedigree, this 30 years of marinating in racial awareness, gave me a simplistic sense that wherever I went—particularly in the "real" world outside of academia—I would assuredly be, or at least come off as, one of the least racist people in the room.

My mother's announcement helped me reflect on the emotional power of racism. Unlike the many women of color I know, work with, and am close friends with and deeply respect, the only thing I knew about this surgeon was her race and gender. My mother didn't start her announcement with "my surgeon went to Johns Hopkins" or "according to [some official ratings] my surgeon has above-average success rates with these very tricky surgeries (where quadra-paralysis is a potential outcome) compared to her peers." No, all I knew about this surgeon was that she was a black woman. And in that moment, that status created doubt and increased my fears.

Reflecting on my reaction, I was additionally surprised to face the fact that her being a woman was a second strike against her! While I might actively seek out a female OB/GYN or pediatrician, somehow one's own (or one's mother's) brain surgeon should be godlike, even arrogant, a man. Hmmmm.

So, what have I learned from all this?

As a micro-experience, it was privately humbling. I was faced with the fact that my education in the dynamics of white privilege and racial oppression, my moral commitments to participating in anti-racism work, and fluency in the language of political correctness are ultimately limited. None of these allows me to transcend the emotional power of racism.

# uh huh!

## alia starkweather

Many, many years ago (maybe 40), I went to swim at the town beach of South Deerfield, Massachusetts, where I was living at the time. I was standing on the beach watching a young interracial couple playing together in the water, stopping to hug and look into each other's eyes occasionally. They were joyful and happy, attractive and having so much fun it was hard not to smile.

I was enjoying them, appreciating the beauty of the dark and light contrast of their bodies, when a white man of middle age came up to me and said, "Isn't that horrible! They should not be allowed here!" or something to that effect. He clearly expected I would feel the way he seemed to feel.

I was stunned. I just looked at him and shrugged in a minimal way, maybe uttering a low "Uh huh" but not wanting to.

Inside I was sick and sad and angry. I was angry at him, but also at myself. Why didn't I tell my truth, or better yet, ask him what he was feeling? What would it have cost me to say, "You sound upset. What is bothering you?" Of course, I never thought of those words but I wished I had at least said, "They are not bothering me. I was enjoying watching them."

Admittedly, I am a slow thinker, but I felt the need to respond to him before I had time to think. When I realized that I had not spoken my truth, I was ashamed and had a sinking feeling inside of me.

I could have said, "I love to watch young people having fun," taking the racial issue out of it all together. I could have said, "We are seeing it differently." Perhaps any one of these answers could have created a dialogue, a conversation. Perhaps we could have learned more about each other. I might have learned more tolerance of him. He might have had new thoughts about the young couple.

Instead, I was complicit. He never knew that I did not agree with him. We never had a chance to learn more about each other, perhaps gaining understanding and respect. Of course, it might have become nasty. He might have gotten angry if I challenged him, however gently. Would I have become angry too? How much did this possibility impede my willingness to answer him honestly? I do wish I could think faster, or perhaps just allow myself time before making a response, so I could really choose the best answer.

But I made a resolution then not to be complicit again. Now I will add another resolution—not to answer quickly if I don't know my best answer right away. I will take time to think and remember all I know about conflict resolution statements, and re-evaluation counseling questions, and allow myself to breathe and be clear.

# a lifelong pull into an unlikely dance

## james wolff

Blessed is the man who does not walk in the counsel of the wicked,
 or stand in the way of sinners,
 or sit in the seat of scoffers....
But his delight is in the word of the Lord
 and on these words he chews day and night,
He is like a tree planted beside streams of water,
 which yields its fruit in season,
 and whose leaves do not wither, whatever he does prospers.
 —Psalm 1:1-3 (New International Version)

You turned my wailing into dancing;
you removed my sackcloth and clothed me with joy,
that my heart may sing to you and not be silent.
O Lord my God, I will give you thanks forever.
 —Ps. 30:11-12. (New International Version)

## SATURDAY, JUNE 7, 2008, MT. PISGAH
## MISSIONARY BAPTIST CHURCH,
## SANDHILL, MISSISSIPPI

Sister Fletcher rose to speak.

"Mr. Clinton Taylor, Sr., the eldest of seven children, was born on November 14, 1929, to the late Noble and Zora Taylor. His sister Mary Mclin (1930) preceded him in death. Clinton was a blessing to everyone with whom. . . ." The words began to shake, sputter, and then they stopped.

"That's alright." The audience assured but not enough to jump-start the stalemate.

"Take your time." Another embrace, but no traction.

Silence. Tears. And now trembling. . . .

The gathering breathed a sigh as another sister stood on cue in the choir loft behind the pulpit. She was in everyone's view. She stood still and erect in the middle of the pew about halfway up into the benches. She spontaneously picked up where the other had ended and read the obituary steadily, calmly, and clearly. Her voice carried a message of stability and strength. There was no need for her to move to the microphone.

"Clinton was a blessing to everyone with whom he came into contact. . . ." Her calm cadence brought a sense that something good was happening. "All who knew him knew that when asked how he was doing, he always said, 'I've never had it so good!'"

Her words swept us upstream. And this is the way of creation.

Words bring form from formlessness (Peterson, 1989). Words bring light and definition into darkness. Words get us moving again when we are stuck. Words bring goodness.

Clinton Taylor's words became the choral response we could all call out this day. "I've never had it so good" became fruit-bearing words pulling us into personal and communal participation in the life of Clinton Taylor.

As the rhythm of his words pulled me in, I also desired to be carried along by their stream. But I knew many at that church did not see me as swimming in their waters. I knew the Taylor family, and they knew me, but many of the people packed into Mt. Pisgah Missionary Baptist Church saw only a white man dressed in a dark suit sitting beside a white woman—presumably his wife.

But it was my turn, and words were all I had. "I have had the privilege of being Mr. Taylor's pastor in Chicago for almost 30 years," I began. "And I invite you to enter into the life he lived by seeing his race, his Bible, and the lives of those who found shelter in his branches through my eyes.

"Now I hesitate to say anything further on the first item," I paused. "...for obvious reasons." A moment of silence followed by emotive laughter. I was wading successfully through currents of color and culture, and now we were all swimming in the same stream.

Clinton Taylor had lived a productive life before I ever met him and long before he returned to Mississippi. For forty years he worked on his five-bedroom bungalow house in the Lawndale community. During that same time, he purchased and rehabbed a three-flat across the street for his children to live in. For most of his life, he was a construction laborer. And most days he wore a laundered blue employee shirt with the wrong name embroidered on it. Every day he worked, he carried a white five-gallon pail with the tools he needed. When he was out of work he found other work. He provided for his wife and a blended family of at least ten.

The community knew his integrity. When the gangs saw him coming, they yielded. He walked to church where he was the repairman. He also served as elder and Sunday School teacher. As a sometimes lonely voice, a Jeremiah, he built, bought, and told fleeing people to stay in the community. Many laughed and ridiculed but Clinton Taylor stood firm. He laid the foundations for a community Christian School, and he saw his dreams bear fruit as a four-million-dollar home for his church and school.

For forty years, Clinton Taylor worked. He worked hard during the day and came home to more, waiting to eat until his tasks were finished. When I first met him, I was a 24-year old student pastor. For the next twenty years, Mr. Taylor was my elder and guide. Shortly after that, he and his wife moved back to Mississippi, and I felt it was time to pay my first visit to see the ground where this great tree originally took root, grew, and flourished.

I left the grey cold of Chicago and headed south just after Thanksgiving. The Mississippi sun still had strength, and it felt good to my skin. While I walked along the gravel road, I noticed a field with scraggly bushes just a little over knee high. A few dirty white clumps of white were hanging on some of the branches. "So that's cotton," I thought, and imagined the story those fields could tell. Pretending I was one of those cotton pickers, I was surprised at how far I had to bend over. The sun was strong but setting early, and I could feel a chill in the air. Though the place surely carried stories of anguish, it also had a calming effect—no cars with loud music blasting out of open windows, no sirens. And the only thieves were rabbits stealing into gardens.

But the waters of Mississippi are muddy, murky, and bitter, and I wondered then as I wonder now how a tree planted besides such a river could live, much less prosper and yield fruit. These waters are toxic, polluted by words of hatred and contempt, segregation, colored and nigger. How can any tree prosper drinking the poisonous waters of betrayal? How could Mr. Taylor be nourished, thrive, and grow to nurture others from such a place?

During that visit, I had a chance to ask him first-hand about this. "Mr. Taylor, how could you leave this quiet place and move into a concrete, crime riddled, and congested place like Chicago?"

"It's really quite simple," he said, "Mississippi was no place for a black man when I was coming up. Today that has changed."

"It is not that changed," quipped Mrs. Taylor.

"Well, yeah Mama, there are always a few bad apples around," Mr. Taylor said, and then he chuckled as he recalled a story. "When I was a teenager, I decided I wanted to go to the race track in Jackson. So I walked up to the man at the counter and said, 'I'll take one ticket.' That man looked at me and said, 'We don't sell tickets to niggers—niggers go in by the horses.'"

"Well," Clint concluded, "that just goes to show you how stupid the man was. I saw the entire race for free and I had a front row seat!"

Then, as now, Mr. Taylor's attitude amazed me. Here was a person who wanted to pay for his seat at the table of the human race, and was forced to take his place with animals—race horses. But when I listened for bitterness, for at least some unleashing of the energy of revenge, it was not there. Rather than stepping toward retribution, Mr. Taylor let the rhythms of grace direct his path.

Mr. Taylor's wisdom came either from the Bible or from his daddy. When it came to dealing with racism, it was his father. "My daddy always said, just because they act stupid, doesn't mean you have to join them."

How can a tree flourish beside such streams? A daddy and horses can help, but Mr. Taylor himself did the growing. He took these words of wisdom, chewed on them and found a way to daily transform them into his own walk.

His walk led him back to where he began. A front row seat with the horses was not his last laugh. Fifty years later he came home to Mississippi, and this time he sat proudly on the porch of his new, freshly painted white wood framed house, looking over five acres. Clinton Taylor, the great-grandson of a slave and a son of a sharecropper now owned the same land on which his ancestors worked horses as slaves. Our country never delivered on its promise of 40 acres and a mule but Mr. Taylor's feet were pulled into a place even more expansive than a ranch home, a place where he became a personal participant dancing to God's melody, which reconciles the world to Himself.

Even in Mississippi—with harsh memories of racetracks and share-croppers—a place where two Americas collided—even in Mississippi the energy of the words of grace could not be stilled.

Clinton Taylor took wisdom from his father, and from his Bible. He used the book, and it showed. Dwight L. Moody used to say that every Bible should be bound in shoe leather (Peterson, 1993). Mr. Taylor's Bible and work boots were both well-worn. And although Mr. Taylor would replace his shoes, whenever the time came, he would simply add another strip of duct-tape to his torn, tattered and Sunday-school-lesson-stuffed Bible. Mr. Taylor's Bible was chewed up! And just as he never had to prove how black he was, neither did he sport What Would Jesus Do? bracelets. He just walked his daily walk, carrying a white, two-gallon pail filled with hammer, crow-bar, right-angle hand-saw and screwdrivers—all anchored by his Bible on the bottom.

Mr. Taylor chewed on the Word. Yet from physical exhaustion, he more often than not would fall asleep during my sermons. In fact, over a twenty year period I don't recall him one time getting excited about anything that I ever preached on. An ego-deflator for any pastor—yet instructive.

I was taught Greek, Hebrew, and infinitive constructs. Mr. Taylor simply read the passage and then attempted to live it. I thought that I needed to study and analyze the stream and all of its ecological context before I would think of swimming in it. Mr. Taylor just jumped in the river feet first! He knew the stream was good, bringing refreshment and buoyancy to his life. Elder Taylor's chewing and jumping taught me the organic unity between the Word read and the Word lived.

While Mr. Taylor did not have a well-formulated theology, his ability to put one foot in front of the other was amazing...and disarming. When the Lawndale church alarm rang in the middle of the night, Mr. Taylor would meet me in front of the church.

"Mr. Taylor, let's wait until the police arrive before going in."

"If God is with us what is there to be afraid of," he replied, as he ran up the front steps and I stood holding the door.

Foolish, irresponsible, crazy—all of the above. Yet it was the irresistible fruit of a good life lived in rhythm with God's Word. An attractiveness which pulled me up the church stairs, too.

The leather of his Bible did not escape the wear and tear of the 1960s. While our higher church assembly exegeted into the early morning hours what Paul's words meant—"All things are lawful for me, but all things are not expedient" (1 Corinthians 10:23, King James Version)—Mr. Taylor's interest was not in what the text meant as much as how it was going to be lived. The debate concerned busing black children to a neighboring white suburb, and for Mr. Taylor, the discussion was anything but abstract. For him it was personal, "Will I be able to send my children to this school?"

In the end, all the lengthy posturing and pontificating mattered little. Mr. Taylor retorted, "What was the use of all that talk, most of the church leaders had their minds made up about what they were going to do before they started." Thus Mr. Taylor experienced firsthand, but not for the first time, the disconnect between the Word read and the Word lived. And while my tradition was strong in the discipline of analyzing abstractly, the leather of Mr. Taylor's faith was as well-worn as his shoes.

Truly, Mr. Taylor's faith helped him to grow and prosper. The tree of his life provided shade and fruit. His life was a kind of "Tree-House Bed and Breakfast" that pulled in birds of every kind! Even strange birds like myself. When I visited that first time, the Taylor kitchen and the Mt. Pisgah Church were large enough for one to nest and eat freely.

And there I was reminded that Jesus and Mrs. Taylor shared a similar story line…fish. For Mrs. Taylor, it was catfish! Hot, moist, with a lightly breaded surface and flakey white flesh inside, sprinkled with a red Tabasco. I loved the shelter of these trees. I ate. Mr. Taylor talked. Mrs. Taylor cooked, grateful to have someone else listening to her husband.

When we went to church together during my first visit, Pisgah's shade proved to be just as protective. I could sense the pride in the Taylors as we went to Sunday school. It was not every day someone could bring their preacher from Chicago.

Now I come from a tradition where a visiting pastor attempts to stay in the background but I knew it was different in the black church. Despite my experience, this made me a bit uneasy, not to mention I was the only white person in attendance.

My fears were not unfounded. "Now we are going to call on our visitor, Rev. Wolff," the minister said, continuing, "I always thought the

85

Taylors came from good stock but now I know they do when I see their preacher come all the way down from Chicago."

I tried to lower the hype about myself and claimed that I came just to eat Mrs. Taylor's catfish and pigs feet. They believed me on the catfish but laughed in disbelief about the pigs feet—all except their pastor.

"Now I've been here for three years and I never had any of those pigs feet!"

As I sat down, relieved to return to the shadow behind the large pulpit, Mr. Taylor shot up out of his pew. With his arm extended and pointing with his finger to give emphasis, he said, "I just want everyone here to know that he wasn't like a lot of these ministers living out in the suburbs and driving in all the time—he and his family lived in the community."

Mr. Taylor's vote of confidence pulled me in further, and I said, "Permit me one story about the community. One night while my family was sleeping, the community crawled through a window. Among other things they helped themselves to a TV, VCR, vacuum cleaner, and adding a final exclamation point, they used my car to move their newly acquired merchandise."

As the country audience gasped at the stereotypes of the big bad city confirmed, Mr. Taylor brought the final word. "And he still did not leave!"

That Sunday afternoon we sat in the shade, enjoying catfish again, and I reminded Mrs. Taylor that now she was going to have to cook for her minister. She laughed, "I ain't having that man over here for no pig's feet."

Shade. Shelter. A strange bird in the Mississippi sun was pulled into a far larger world than the Pisgah and Taylor hospitality. This was a surprise pull into participating as a partner in a community created by God's movement.

And many others found enough space in these branches to place their nest.

Ten years later, the day I rose to speak in his honor, Mr. Taylor had 67 children, grand and great-grandchildren gathered under his tree, not to mention all the others who had squeezed under the shelter of the Mt. Pisgah roof.

"In the end, what makes a man prosperous?" I asked, "How does one measure the value of one's life—houses, land, investments?"

"No, not by how tall the tree is, for some trees rise very high yet provide little shelter. No, their value is in their branches. Limbs that are expansive and strong enough to invite birds of every kind to find a place and flourish—participating and contributing in the prosperity of life. Look around you and see all the birds that have found a nest in the branches of Mr. Taylor's tree."

"Pastor Wolff," a voice came from behind me as I walked back from the grave dug in the reddish ground nestled under the trees not fifty yards from the church. I turned and saw in the distance three of Mr. Taylor's grandsons coming my way. Their ground was very different from their grandfather's. Theirs was not of dirt but of concrete. Most of their energy was being put into finding any soil fertile enough to grow in and to become more than a seedling before being mowed down. Their threat was not the racetrack man telling them to go "in with the horses" because they found themselves already in the stall.

"Pastor Wolff," Johnythan, the one I knew best spoke for the three. "Man, did you ever get granddaddy right...you made it for us!" All three gave me a brother-to-brother handshake and hug.

I fumbled for something to say because I knew then that my previous words had crossed the goal line. "It's not hard to say good things about good people. Besides how many pastors can say they knew someone for 30 years."

A preacher's tools are words. When there is a congruency between the words of our lives and the Word of Life, trees prosper—including the pastor's. It is an amazing event when the Holy Spirit connects the Word read with the Word lived. It can also be humorous. The grandsons were partially laughing as they embraced me...chuckling...because I was white. I was not supposed to connect. While black people have been forced to adapt to white society, for the most part white people have not returned the favor. I did not fit into their landscape, yet I had paid close enough attention to the way things were arranged to be added and embraced.

I was embraced yet continued to catch glances. As I sat with my wife at Mt. Pisgah, Asia, the 7- year old great-granddaughter of Mr. Taylor's, sat three pews in front of us. Her hair pressed and curled, curiously peering just above the top edge of her pew, caught my attention after I saw her dark eyes staring at us for the fourth time. Asia was in the first grade and attended our church's school in Chicago. She was accustomed to seeing me and my wife. White people fit for her in Chicago at school and church but not at Mt. Pisgah, in Mississippi. What were we doing there? Already, at seven, she was asking the question we had asked ourselves over the past 30 years. What were we doing there? Johnythan's laugh and Asia's glance, two who had found the shelter of Mr. Taylor's tree, helped move us closer to some clarity.

The branches from Taylor's tree had built a strong bridge across a crevasse cutting across our nation's history. The branches were strong enough to connect the incongruent worlds—of Jim Crow's cotton and Johnythan's Chicago, of Asia's precociousness and our puzzlement. While Mr. Taylor did not remove the chasm, his broad branches spanned far enough for us to travel back and forth.

How does one recognize a prosperous tree? By the lives pulled its way. Taylor's life was a long pull in the same direction (Peterson, 1980). When solid trees and satisfying streams intersect, a pleasing product appears. The result of God's words absorbed into living, as a fine grain is seamlessly embedded in wood, is a beautiful life. An attractiveness is loosed that will not be ignored. An aroma bypassers cannot resist pulls them into participation.

Including this pastor. The life and joy of this "tree planted beside streams of water" rekindled my passion for the two lovers who originally attracted me to ministry: God's Word and God's People. Correct that, I really had only one lover I wanted to actually live with—the story, the story of God's word breathing life into the seemingly ordinary lives of God's people—the story of the Trinity's "will being done on earth as it is in heaven." My heart has longed to hear, to touch, and to see what for the most part is inaudible, untouchable, and invisible. But the eye wanders, and pastors rather than being pulled into the way which leads to life, push their way onto the Olympic awards platform of "pastors you should know." The adrenalin high of swank sanctuaries filled with burgeoning bodies swelling the church's billfolds is too intoxicating for pastors to push back from.

On top of this, despite our deepest desires, we find ourselves courting other sweethearts. Our mistresses demand surrender to the ways of the world. The small, the nuanced detail, have little appeal. They want a big rock! Big plans are insisted on, so that they too may be lifted out of the ordinary. The pull is strong and seductive but if pastors surrender to this way, they perish.

Pastors work with ordinary trees. God hands us the seemingly small and often invisible details of story. Ours is the task of uncovering the gift in the give-ness. For the most part, what we do will go unnoticed and we will need to develop habits which intentionally disappoint our mistresses all the while acting as a tour guide, accenting what appears to be a plain landscape into a scene that comes alive with the energetic God. Our job is to show the "ordinary sacred" (Peterson, 1989, p. 50).

John Calvin frequently refers to creation as a "theater of God's glory" (Peterson, 1989). This arena gives us "a good look" (Greek-theatron) and we see that everything carries the signature of the Creator. Pastors are given the theater of the narrative: God's stories and people's stories. And pastors have been gifted with the task of paying close attention to His signature on both—believing the words of God, as in the beginning, continue to breathe life into the *tohu* and *bohu* (translated from the Hebrew as formless and empty—Genesis 1:2).

I don't have much rhythm. In fact, on the dance floor, I am a hopeless white man, the very embodiment of *tohu* and *bohu*. But the black community pulled me on the floor and patiently showed me that there was rhythm hidden deep within us all. They taught me by inviting me into the narratives of their lives, and I was pulled into the dance.

89

And this dance is not exclusively ours; it is a Trinitarian dance....The Father, Son, and Holy Ghost moving "swiftly with and between and among one another...holding on and letting go...making it impossible at times to distinguish one person from another." God is alive "creating, saving, and blessing" (Peterson, 2005, p. 45). God calls us in the everyday, to participate in His dance. Pastors are pulled daily and pulling others to participate in this dance—the Word read and the Word lived. The Trinity's words link arm in arm with the participant's words, and pastors have the privilege to use both, in order to breathe life into the dance.

Why did Mr. Taylor's life pull me and others into the dance? The primary pull was not because he had made it out of the sweltering kitchen of Mississippi to taste a piece of the American pie, nor because he could articulate clearly this week's Sunday school lesson. No, he pulled us into the Way with his story. His narrative segued into God's, a life melded to the dance.

His was a long dance; the pull of one whose dignity was betrayed by a nation worshiping color more than persons; the pull of one who learned the difficult steps of reconciliation instead of seeking revenge; the pull of one who finished with the energy and power of forgiveness. Clinton Taylor's story pulls us into God's life-giving streams.

And it pulled me into an unlikely dance, a dance whose rhythms appeared to be chaotic, contrapuntal, even subversive, a dance with an ever-present hand inviting me to a partnership of movement that is far larger than I could have imagined on my own (Peterson, 2005). This dance invited me to set aside what I was doing and partner in what God was doing—Father, Son, and Holy Spirit calling me "to participate in the energetically active life of God" (Peterson, 2005, p. 46).

Mr. Taylor's life was a long pull in the same direction.... Not only did I get a front row seat, I got to dance.

Walk with me and work with me—watch how I do it.

Learn the unforced rhythms of grace.

I won't lay anything heavy or ill-fitting on you.

Keep company with me and you'll learn to live freely and lightly.
—Matthew 11:29-30. (*The Message*)

---

*Footnotes*

1. In his book, *Christ Plays in Ten Thousand Places: A conversation in spiritual theology*, Peterson stated that John Damascene in the 8th century used this metaphor for the trinity. The Greek word, Perichoresis, is broken down into Peri=around and choresis=dance.

---

*References*

Peterson, E. H. (1989). *Answering God*. New York, NY: Harper Collins.

Peterson, E. H. (1980). *A long obedience in the same direction*. Downers Grove, IL: Intervarsity Press.

Peterson, E. H. (2005). *Christ plays in ten thousand places: A conversation in spiritual theology*. Grand Rapids, MI: Eerdmans Publishing Co.

Peterson, E. Hl (2005). *The Message: The Bible in Contemporary Language*. NewPress Publishing Group.

This article first appeared on the website, "Resources for American Christianity" at http://www.resourcingchristianity.org.

# the size of the shackles

## tim ahrens

A few years ago, while diving off the coast of Africa, scuba divers discovered a slave ship buried in a watery grave. Not many of these ships have been found because the motivation for finding them is low. They carried no gold. Their treasure was human cargo. Like pirate ships, they carried few records or logs.

The divers discovered many things in the watery grave including tiny, little bracelet-like shackles no more than one inch across. Historians noted they finally had evidence of what they thought to be true—African babies and infants who were brought from Africa to America in shackles.

The image of shackled babies as slaves has often overwhelmed me when considering the 300-year experience of African people on American soil. Stealing people from their homes, shackling, transporting, selling and enslaving free men, women, and children from Africa's west coast to America's east coast was the most treacherous and evil industry ever conceived and perpetrated by humanity against humanity. It was largely a crime of white men against black humanity, and it continued for hundreds of years. If you were to drain the Atlantic Ocean, the bones of the millions who died in transit would point the way to our American coastline.

The shackled bones of babies still lie on the Atlantic Ocean floor. Although we in America would like to bury the chains and the memories of slavery, we must deal with this horrible heritage which will not rest in peace until we do. Senator Obama's speech on "Race in America" given in March 2008 while standing by the Liberty Bell in Philadelphia as well as Rev. Dr. Jeremiah Wright's provocative and disturbing words shake us at a deep level because we have yet to fully embrace the memories of the primal and pivotal experience of African Americans.

Here is what we can do. We can sit and listen. We can hear the stories of the living and their stories of the dead with their experience of racial oppression and pain. We can hear the stories of men and women who have known the sting of prejudice and felt the residual pain of racism. If you listen long enough and build relationships deep enough with those who have known this pain, they will tell of the millions. They will tell of their grandparents' lynchings and great-grandparents in slavery. They will tell of their children coming home in tears asking why they were hated because of the color of their skin. They will tell you about the murder of youth and children during the civil rights movement. You will hear of the murder of Emmett Till in 1955 and Addie Mae Collins, Denise McNair, Carole Robinson and Cynthia Wesley in 1963, who were blown up in the women's room of the 16th St. Baptist Church in Birmingham as they prepared to go to worship.

We can also experience this story ourselves. Everyone who reads this must go the Martin Luther King, Jr. Center in Columbus, Ohio and spend time in the Goree Island exhibition. It contains the sights and sounds of the experience of passing through "the door of no return" through which generations of free people passed on their way out of Africa and into slavery. This visceral experience of entering into the *Maafa*—the great suffering—will change you.

There is a saying: "the way out is back through." I believe we must go back through this experience again and again until it is paradoxically purged and embedded in our soul.

In his book *Race Matters*, Cornel West writes that overcoming the experience of racism in America will take a spirit like jazz. We need to become jazz people of faith. Jazz is the ability to improvise, to be fluid, to be flexible, to be suspicious of "either/or" viewpoints. Jazz doesn't trust the ruts of dogmatic pronouncements. It won't stay still for liberal/conservative mindsets. To move through the music, you have to integrate and galvanize dissonant tones and voices in a creative tension which actually yields a much higher level of performance. I believe Jesus was jazz when he faced racism and hostilities in his context. May we become jazz people of faith as we embrace creative tension. Then we can sing in a new voice: "We shall overcome someday."

# talkin' the talk

## savanna ouellette

The Cedar Rapids airport was sparsely populated when my colleague, Cynthia, and I flew into Iowa on a business trip. As we waited for the hotel shuttle to pick us up, we watched an African-American man sweeping the floor of the terminal. Cynthia, a Jamaican-born black woman, remarked that she felt such a sense of isolation in this white, Midwestern city that she experienced an immediate bond with the maintenance man working inside. I had been worried about her sense of comfort in Iowa since we left the Northeast but hadn't decided how to talk about it. With her usual sense of humor intact, she proceeded to make jokes about her chances of emerging unscathed from the coming two-day training we were to deliver to a group of social workers.

The next day I was prepared to support Cynthia in the face of hostility at worst and silent stares at best. The group consisted of twenty or so foster care workers from various surrounding towns and, as expected, there was not one dark face in the crowd. After brief introductions, Cynthia launched into the first part of her presentation. I had neglected to take into account that she has a charming Jamaican accent and is a very experienced presenter so that within fifteen minutes, everyone was participating, laughing at her jokes, and seemed to be hanging on every word. I had clearly made an error in judgment about those Iowans which was, no doubt, based on my own prejudiced expectations.

Later, as I reflected on why my worst fears had not materialized, I wondered if one of the factors in Cynthia's acceptance as a trainer, in Iowa or anywhere else, had something to do with her language patterns. It seems that a charming accent can go a long way in making someone who is different more acceptable.

I was reminded of my college days when I was a member of a club for foreign and American students. One of the students was from South Africa and she also had a very engaging speech pattern. All of the native English speakers tried to engage her in conversation just to hear the musicality of her voice. She did very well with all of her classmates and did not experience any prejudice in general. On the other hand, an African-American young woman member of our group often struggled with what she perceived as racist attitudes.

What conclusion can be drawn from these experiences? Although being different can often be seen as a liability in a group, it seems that language can be an asset when it is unique. Why then are African-American language patterns not appreciated by white society? Why does Bill Cosby tell parents to teach their children to speak "acceptable" English and not black "slang"? Could it be that the media makes that form of communication seem dangerous? Are we being programmed to fear everything that is associated with non-middle class African-American culture? If we go back to the music scene in the 1960s, we see the same phenomenon with tame, white groups covering songs that had been previously recorded by black artists. Those recordings were thought too raw, too dangerous by record distributors so they had to be sanitized and made palatable for sale to a white public.

There are, of course, much deeper attitudes underlying the institutional racism which exists in the United States today. It would be naïve to think that changing speech patterns could affect how African Americans are viewed in this country. We will need to continue the struggle to change attitudes and behaviors until every person is respected and valued. In the meantime, I will enjoy working with Cynthia and make every effort to not underestimate our audiences.

the start of new conversations

# jesus and jeremiah

## vicki kemper

EDITORS' NOTE
The Reverend Kemper preached the following sermon at the First
Congregational Church in Amherst, Massachusetts, U.C.C. on May 18,
2008. The sermon and the entire worship service were designed to initi-
ate a series of Sacred Conversations on Race. The United Church of
Christ called for a dialogue on race in response to criticism and political
distortions of some remarks made by the Reverend Dr. Jeremiah Wright.
The scripture references are to Jeremiah 6:13-14 and 7:1-8.

As we gather together this morning to begin what we hope will be a series
of sacred conversations on race, it seems to me that the real issue is not
so much what we will say today, but rather what we will hear. Of course,
that is the key question whenever we come before our still-speaking
God—whenever we gather for worship, whenever we study the scriptures, whenever we pray together.

We come longing to encounter the Holy. We yearn to be touched by
the God who is love, filled with the power of the Spirit, challenged and

encouraged by the radical compassion and loving acceptance of our brother Jesus. Today and every time we gather we want to hear good news—news of hope and healing, words of wisdom and comfort, the gospel of forgiveness and belonging.

And yet I am aware that many of us came to worship this morning with somewhat wary, even heavy, hearts. It has been an unsettling couple of weeks: First the massive cyclone in Myanmar, where human cruelty is adding to the massive suffering caused by a natural disaster. Then the massive earthquake in China, where that nation's relative openness to the outside world has allowed our hearts to be broken by the pictures and sounds of collapsed schools, wailing parents, and death and devastation on a scale beyond our comprehension.

There is among many of us an unsettling sense of the world falling apart. We consider unfathomable suffering, we ponder the fragility of life, and we wonder where God is—if God is—in it all. And so, perhaps even more than usual, we come longing to hear God's good news.

But this is the day we have committed ourselves to talking about race, of all things. This is the day we have devoted to the discussion of a painful, challenging, and discomforting issue. And so the question is what we will hear. We know what we want to hear: good news. And we believe God has good news for us. But what is the good news when it comes to race? Is there any good news?

When we consider that white "racism is rooted in a 400-year-old system of economic exploitation,"[1] and concede that economic exploitation of all types is still very much with us—"from the least to the greatest of them, everyone is greedy for unjust gain," our scripture says—it is easy to feel discouraged.

When we consider that "the average net worth of white families in 2008 remains 10 times greater than the average net worth of black families, [that] racial segregation in our public schools has intensified,"[2] that affirmative action policies are under attack, that one out of every four African Americans lives in poverty, and that African Americans have shorter life spans, get longer prison sentences, and live altogether more complicated, difficult lives than whites, it is easy to feel overwhelmed and disempowered.

When we consider that many African Americans suffer from what one expert calls "protracted traumatic stress disorder,"[3] the ongoing racial discrimination and daily diminishments that continue to damage the African-American psyche, weakening the black family and community, it is easy to feel hopeless.

When we consider white privilege—the untold, largely-taken-for-granted benefits we have as the dominant, majority population in this country—it is easy to end up feeling either ashamed and confused or guilty and angry.

Of course, given our natural needs for comfort and reassurance, our human tendencies toward denial and repression, we don't want to consider any of those things. We would rather focus on the positive; we would rather talk about how far we've come. After all, racial segregation and the denial of equal rights in voting, housing and health care were the law of the land as recently as 40, 50 years ago[4] and now we've nominated an African American to be president of the United States. We feel pretty good about that!

We are tempted to listen to the false prophets who—despite all the evidence of enduring racist attitudes, institutions and conditions—would treat carelessly our nation's original wound, saying, "Peace, peace," when there is no peace. Given how hard peace is to find, given how desperately we need to hear a good word, we are tempted to trust in their deceptive words. We are tempted to believe that our politically correct views, openness to all, and proud history cover a multitude of sins and absolve us of responsibility for ongoing inequities. In the false security of our false peace we may have settled for being non-racist instead of answering God's call to work against racism, to commit ourselves to moving beyond race-based roles, to restoring relationships, reconciling communities, and dismantling the institutions of racism.

But injustice is absolute, not relative. Racism that persists in attitudes and systems is no less unjust than racism that is written into law.

The racial discrimination encountered by a young African-American woman is no less dehumanizing because her grandparents could not vote; the young man pulled over by the police for driving-while-black does not experience less humiliation because his father could not get even a job that paid enough to get a loan to buy a car.

And yet the false prophets of our time say "Justice, justice" when there is no justice; they say "Progress, progress" when we have far to go. The false prophets of our time say, "Come, let us worship God; Come, let us delight in God's goodness and celebrate our goodness," all the while ignoring the suffering and injustice that surrounds us—oppression that God calls us to end; division and enmity that God calls us to address; sisters and brothers with whom God calls us to reconcile.

So where is the good news? Where is the hope? Is there any good news when we talk about race?

God knows there is. But as always, we cannot put our hope in circumstances or our good intentions or human wisdom; not even a history of good deeds and right actions is enough to overcome present evils and create a better future. Hope based on nothing more than a vague, optimistic "sense that things are going to get better" is sure to disappoint us. Instead, our hope must be "rooted in nothing other than God's promise" to do a new thing in us and through us.[5] And it is only in expressing our grief about current conditions that we can engage in faith-based, "hope-filled action for the future."[6]

The good news we seek is all around us in the love of God and our common relationship with the God of love. The good news is our shared identity as children of God and the hope of coming into the fullness of our humanity by the grace of God's all-inclusive love. The good news is the joy of living into our life's purpose of being in relationship with God, the healing that comes from working for God's justice, the richness of our life together as God's community, and the exhilaration of fulfilling God's call to be agents of reconciliation.

The good news God speaks to us today is that "our deepest common humanity is not grounded in race, religious creed, or national origin but in the extravagantly inclusive love of God."[7] We can find good, healing news in African-American spirituality and in the African concept of *ubuntu*, which reminds us that we become fully human only in community with one another.

We know the good news in the story of Joseph, whose brothers sold him into slavery, and who later rose to a position from which he saved their lives and a remnant of Israel. We see in that story the good news that we can be saved by our reconciliation with those we have oppressed. We know from the story of Joseph and his brothers the good news that what humans intend for evil God can use for good.

And so it is that a cynical, racist political agenda designed to seriously weaken the presidential campaign of Barack Obama by mocking his former pastor has created a new opportunity for movement toward racial healing and reconciliation. Because of the racist elements of the political attacks on Rev. Jeremiah Wright, the United Church of Christ and the National Council of Churches called on their member congregations to have a national preach-in today on race and to hold sacred conversations on race.

And so it is that we and so many other congregations are setting out on a challenging and exciting journey, answering God's "high and holy calling"[8] to love our neighbors as ourselves, to be in right relationship with God and all God's children.

Consider this: If only one-quarter of the U.C.C. congregations are talking about race today, the journey to reconciliation is beginning in almost 1,400 churches across our country. If just half of U.C.C. churches are having sacred conversations about race today, God's light is shining more brightly in almost 2,800 places in our land. And if just one person in each of those congregations has a change of heart; if just one person from each church reaches out to an African-American neighbor or colleague; if just one group from each congregation commits itself to working against racism, we will be thousands and thousands of steps closer to the Beloved Community God intended for us.

And that is good news!

*Footnotes*

1. Herbert Perkins and Margery Otto, "Principles and Assumptions Underlying a Conversation on Race," www.ucc.org.

2. The United Church of Christ Collegium of Officers, "A Pastoral Letter on Racism," www.ucc.org.

3 Lee H. Butler Jr., *A Loving Home: Caring for African American Marriage and Families* (Cleveland: The Pilgrim Press, 2000).

4 "Steps for Starting the Conversation," www.ucc.org.

5 Walter Brueggemann, *Like Fire in the Bones* (Minneapolis: Fortress Press, 2006), 182.

6 Ibid., 188.

7 "A Pastoral Letter on Racism," op. cit.

8 Ibid.

# where to begin?

## sarah buteux

EDITORS' NOTE
The Reverend Sarah Buteux preached the following sermon on May 18, 2008 at the First Congregational Church of Hadley, Massachusetts, U.C.C.

> Not everything that is faced can be changed.
> But nothing can be changed until it is faced.
> —James Baldwin

In the beginning...things were a mess. I keep telling myself this because it makes me feel better. In the beginning...things were a mess. The earth was formless and void, dark and empty. Which is not to say that there was nothing or in any way imply that what was before was in some way bad.

There was, according to Genesis, most definitely something, and it was potentially good, but there was nothing nice and neat or even vaguely manageable about the something that was in the beginning.

Before light there was darkness. Before earth and sky and the oceans they define, there was the deep, a sort of formless, chaotic, fathomless, primordial stew of possibility. The deep was like a great cosmic womb. "Not barren," to quote Wayne Muller, "but pregnant, an emptiness teeming with the promise of (new) life."

And I like that image, because I know a little something about pregnancy and birth, and I can tell you that although it may be beautiful, beautiful isn't the same thing as pretty. Bringing new life into the world is messy. My guess is that beginnings always are.

Precipitated by the media frenzy surrounding the Rev. Jeremiah Wright and a sermon he preached seven years ago at Trinity United Church of Christ, we in the United Church of Christ have been charged by the Rev. John Thomas—the president of the U.C.C.—to begin not just any conversation, but a sacred conversation about race in our churches. This is no easy task.

In fact, I think if we are going to do this, even if we do it well, it is bound to be messy. I'm going to do my best to speak the truth in love, but I have no doubt that with a topic this delicate, I'm still going to mess this up and say something that offends someone or fail to say something I should have said. And so I beg your patience and appeal to your grace because whenever we talk about race, especially here in America, it's messy.

And yet, it needs to be done, because you see, the more I've thought about all of it, the more I've realized how long overdue this conversation really is, not just in our nation or even in this church, but in my life in particular. And I have to tell you, that last realization really surprised me.

I confess to you that my first response when I heard about this challenge was a sort of naive excitement. You see, I love being a part of the U.C.C. precisely because it is such a progressive denomination. Historically, our church has been at the forefront of social justice movements, prophetically stepping out of line with mainstream American culture to work for the abolition of slavery, women's rights, desegregation, racial reconciliation, gay rights, immigration reform, and peace. (And that's the short list.)

We can totally do this, I thought, because we've been doing this all along. We here in the U.C.C., surrounded as we are by such a great cloud of witnesses, can not only begin these conversations about race, but serve as a model for other churches and communities who would love to do this sort of thing but wouldn't even know where to begin.

Now, I'm not a total idiot. I knew that our church here in Hadley was predominantly white, not entirely but predominantly, and I confess to you all that I had resigned myself to this fact rather early on in my ministry here, rationalizing that Hadley itself was mostly white and there wasn't much I could do about that. And I was wrong.

Whenever I find myself rationalizing, I usually am. However, the larger church is much more diverse, I thought. If we've got the will then we certainly have the resources. I just need to connect up with my colleagues and they'll help shepherd me through this process.

Well, very soon after Rev. Thomas issued his challenge, I gathered with the other U.C.C. pastors in Western Massachusetts for what they call "A Day of Covenant." We all sat down in a circle, agreed that the sacred conversation about race was at the top of our list of things to talk about, and then looked around the room at our gathering and realized that there was not one person of color in the entire room. "Hmmm," I thought to myself, "this may be a little harder than I thought."

I then started to simply keep my eyes open and really look at my life, the people I work with, my community, and how we all align ourselves. I met with the Hampshire clergy group, attended my new clergy group, went to my lectionary study group, called to mind everyone I knew in my Amherst clergy group...all white. Not so good.

During this time, we visited Amherst College to hear a steel drum ensemble from Trinidad, and as I looked around at the crowd I thought, this is more like it. There were students and faculty of various ages, colors, and nationalities all hanging out together and listening to the music.

Everyone was happy. Things were cool. It was great. And I spent some time wondering what the college has figured out that the church hasn't. But then, just two days later, I attended a party of Amherst faculty, a small, private affair, and once again, of the 40 or so people there, I'm pretty sure everyone in the room was white.

Now why am I telling you all this? Well, I'm telling you all this because in my mind, as necessary as I thought it was for us to begin having this sacred conversation about race—here in this church and across our country—I confess I thought it was a heck of a lot more necessary for some people than others. And I definitely thought I was on the less necessary end of the spectrum.

I went to Smith and Harvard, for goodness' sake, places where they drill diversity training into you as a matter of course. But up until now, up until I really began to examine myself—the assumptions I live with and my life—the advantages I take for granted everyday as a white, able-bodied, heterosexual, married, upper middle class, mainline Protestant woman living in a nice, safe, academic town on the East coast of the wealthiest nation in the world, I didn't think of myself as part of the problem and I certainly didn't think of myself as racist.

But the more I thought about all of this, the more I read and the more I looked around me, the more I realized just how deeply complicit I am in a culture that systematically withholds privilege from some in order to directly benefit people who live and look just like me. At which point I realized that I needed help, and so I called upon people in our church to get me back on the right track.

Glen Franklin, in particular, was a big help. He and I went out to lunch a few weeks ago to talk about all of this and he suggested I read Beverly Tatum's brilliant little book, *Why Are All the Black Kids Sitting Together in the Cafeteria?* It was very eye opening. You see, I had learned all about institutionalized racism back in college, and then I had conveniently forgotten about it because the truth is, as a white woman in our society, I don't really need to remember.

I had gradually regressed, in spite of my education, preferring once again to define racism simply as acts or words deliberately meant to hurt someone of a different color, which is something I would never intentionally do, which makes it easy to forget that racism has anything to do with me.

Reading Tatum's work, I was reminded that racism isn't just actively hurting or alienating someone who doesn't look like you. Racism is not simply prejudice. Racism is "a system of advantage based on race." And here in the United States, according to Tatum: "Every social indicator, from salary to life expectancy, reveals the advantages of being white."

Does this mean all whites are racist? No, but it does mean that all whites benefit from the history and effects of racism that are alive and well in our society, whether we realize it or not. And unless we are consciously working against these forces, that is unless we are part of the solution, well, as the old saying goes, then we are still part of the problem.

"We teach what we were taught," says Beverly Tatum. "The unexamined prejudices of parents are passed on to their children. It is not our fault, but it is our responsibility to interrupt this cycle."

Tatum goes on to describe the institution of racism as one of those moving walkways you see in the airport, which I found to be a very useful image. She says: "Active racist behavior (such as identifying as a white supremacist or calling people derogatory names), is equivalent to walking fast on the conveyor belt. Passive racist behavior (such as laughing at racist jokes or turning a blind eye toward exclusionary hiring practices) is equivalent to standing still on the walkway."

Her point is that as a white person you don't have to do anything to benefit from racism, but even if you do nothing, you still advance down the walkway. That's how pervasive and insidious this whole thing is. What is needed is for white people to stop standing still, turn around, (which in my mind is a beautiful image of repentance) and start actively and intentionally walking in the opposite direction.

The relevant question is not whether all whites are racist (she says), but how we can move more white people from a position of active or passive racism to one of active anti-racism? The task of interrupting racism is obviously not the task of whites alone (she says). But the fact of white privilege means that whites have greater access to the societal institutions that need to change. To whom much is given, much is required.

Well, I couldn't have said it better myself. As I read Tatum's book, I began to realize that it's really not enough to just sit around and think that racism is wrong and wish it wasn't a reality, which is pretty much what I've been doing all these years.

You actually have to work against it, interrupt it, call it when you see it, confess it when you're complicit in it, and remind yourself over and over and over again that we are all created in God's image. No one deserves more than anyone else and certainly no one deserves less. This world was created for us all, because all of us, all of us, are created in the image of God.

Are you with me? Do you think I'm nuts? Exaggerating? Making more of all this then I should? I hope not. I hope you're all still with me and that deep in your heart you are asking yourself what you can do, whatever the color of your skin, the reality of your ancestry or your place in society, to work against this evil.

Because, my friends, that walkway is powerful, and it's been running a really long time, leaving way too many people behind, inflicting wounds too deep for words, and dehumanizing all of us in the process. And I'll tell you what. The more I think about this, the more I want to know what it's going to take, not just to start walking in the opposite direction but to throw a wrench in the works? I don't just want to learn how to walk against the tide. Ultimately, I want to know what we can do to fully dismantle the system.

And yes, I know I'm getting ahead of myself. I know it's going to take time and I know it's going to be hard, and if we begin here and now in this church, even just talking about it, I know it's going to get messy, but with the help of God we can do this because God knows how to work with messy. If the Bible is any indication, God's been doing so right along. In fact, God's been at work right here in Hadley opening doors and laying the foundation for this conversation before I even knew we were going to have it. Let me tell you a little story.

You know that Fifth Sunday thing we started back in September? Well as part of that day we've been preparing and delivering food over to the Amherst Survival Center, and as a result, I got to talking with people there about how we might get more involved beyond just dropping off food and supplies.

Not only that, after reading about our work in the Hampshire Gazette, other churches have stepped up and started doing the Fifth Sunday thing too, so they've been calling the Survival Center as well to see what they can do.

Well they've got some pretty smart people working over there in Amherst and they know a good thing when they see it, so they went over to a little place called Class Action—this amazing organization that exists right here in Hadley to help raise awareness about how the forces of racism and classism and sexism and a whole host of other isms intersect to keep people in poverty, and asked them for advice.

"We've got all this energy coming from the churches right now," they said. "How can we harness it and start making some real institutional changes?"

Well, the people at Class Action called on the ministers in the area who started the Fifth Sunday Project and we sat down and talked. Then they wrote a grant to the Women's Fund of Massachusetts, and right after Easter we were awarded—are you ready for this?—more than thirty-seven thousand dollars to help us get people from our various churches together with the people who depend on the services over at the Survival center so that we can sit down around the same table and start talking about how we can work together to make things better.

The people at Class Action have the tools and the training to facilitate these discussions and we are going to kick off this program right here in our church. There will be food and child care and people coming from Amherst and Haydenville and Northampton and who knows where else, and together—rich and poor, black and white, Latino and Asian, able-bodied and differently-abled, young and old, gay and straight—we are going to get to know one another and I do believe we are going to make a difference.

And I've got to tell you that I think this is just amazing. Right here in our church we'll be able to start having these conversations that we so desperately need to have, conversations about racism and classism and sexism and all those other isms that are fueling that damned walkway and keeping people down.

I earnestly believe that if we can sit down together and talk openly and honestly with one another, then we will find ways to throw a wrench in the works of oppression and start constructing something new and beautiful and life-giving, a little something Jesus used to talk about and Dr. King used to preach about called the beloved community.

We can do this, my friends, and we can do this well. Yes, it's going to be hard, and no doubt it's going to be messy, but we are being called and I do believe that we are able. To whom much has been given—and we have been given a lot—much is required.

I'd like to close by re-reading the passage we heard earlier from Paul's Letter to the Romans. Knowing what you know now, hear these words again, because right here in our scriptures is the blueprint we need to start our sacred conversation and heal this beautiful, bent, and broken world. Paul writes:

> Therefore, I urge you, brothers and sisters, in view of God's mercy, to offer yourselves as living sacrifices, holy and pleasing to God—this is your spiritual act of worship. Do not conform any longer to the pattern of this world, but be transformed by the renewing of your mind. Do not think of yourself more highly than you ought, but rather think of yourself with sober judgment, in accordance with the measure of faith God has given you.
>
> Just as each of us has one body with many members, and these members do not all have the same function, so in Christ we who are many form one body, and each member belongs to all the others.
>
> We all have different gifts, according to the grace

given us. If a person's gift is prophesying, let them use it in proportion to their faith. If it is serving, let them serve; if it is teaching, let them teach; if it is encouraging, let them encourage; if it is contributing to the needs of others, let them give generously; if it is leadership, let them govern diligently; if it is showing mercy, let them do it cheerfully.

I think what Paul is saying is that we all need each other and we all need to do our part. He then finishes up with these words:

Love must be sincere. Hate what is evil; cling to what is good. Be devoted to one another in brotherly love. Honor one another above yourselves. Never be lacking in zeal, but keep your spiritual fervor, serving the Lord. Be joyful in hope, patient in affliction, and faithful in prayer. Share with God's people who are in need. Practice hospitality. Bless those who persecute you; bless and do not curse. Rejoice with those who rejoice; mourn with those who mourn. Live in harmony with one another. Do not be proud, but be willing to associate with people of low position. Do not be conceited. Do not repay anyone evil for evil. Be careful to do what is right in the eyes of everybody. If it is possible, as far as it depends on you, live at peace with everyone. Do not take revenge, my friends, but leave room for God's wrath, for it is written: "It is mine to avenge; I will repay," says the Lord. On the contrary: "If your enemy is hungry, feed him; if he is thirsty, give him something to drink. In doing this, you will heap burning coals on his head." Do not be overcome by evil, but overcome evil with good.

# the legacy of slavery for white people today

## russ vernon-jones

I've had a good number of opportunities to listen to African Americans about their struggles with distress recordings passed down to them by ancestors, and clearly come from the horrible hurts of slavery. As a result, I've wondered what was passed down to me—a white person—from that time.

As far as I know, I don't have slave-owners in my lineage, but I certainly have white ancestors who were living in the United States (or the colonies before that) who were part of the culture that condoned and accepted slavery. I've had a number of sessions (talking, crying with grief, and shaking with fear) about what those white ancestors of mine must have felt and believed, and how those views are reflected in me and in other white people around me.

In my view, this is a partial list of what white people living in the United States at the time of slavery felt, believed and did in order to emotionally and mentally accept the complete subjugation of people from Africa.

- They had to desensitize or blind themselves to the

pain and dehumanization that the enslaved people of African heritage experienced. I assume this happened primarily through seeing the enslaved as not fully human, creating a self-deluding illusion about the realities of enslaved people's lives or simply refusing to look at, see, or think about what was happening.

• They had to feel a disconnection from people with darker skin.

• They feared the anger of people of African heritage because of what was being done in slavery.

• They assumed that what they wanted or needed as white people was more important than the needs of people of African heritage, that white people mattered more than black people.

• They called black people shiftless, and told themselves they work hard only when white people make them work.

• They believed that the economic inequality of slavery was necessary for the economy to thrive and for white people to maintain their wealth.

• They assumed that white people were superior, more intelligent, more reliable, etc. when compared to people of African heritage.

We know that harmful ideas, distressed feelings, and rigidities in people's thinking are often passed on from generation to generation. As much as I don't want to admit it, I can see elements of most of the items on this list in my own mind and feelings today. As much as I reject these notions, I have to acknowledge that some form of them resides somewhere in my mind. I also see them in the foreign policy of our nation with regard to situations involving people with dark skin around the world, as well as in our domestic policies.

My work on this has helped spur me to get rid of the legacy of slavery as it exists in me. But there's another, somewhat surprising result of this work. I find myself interested in working with white people around the elimination of racism. I always knew that work with other white people was important, but it never really appealed to me. Now I'm actively interested in connecting with other white people around these issues, including whites that don't see things the way I do. I've started organizing with some white friends to reach out to other whites about it. We're listening to each other and connecting in new ways already.

# just listen

## jay elliott

There are times these days when I feel the need to find some respite amidst the ruckus and chaos of the world as it streams racial discourses at me through computer monitor, radio, and flatscreen TV. The twenty-four-hour news cycle, the blogosphere, and the political campaigns present race in images, words, and concepts that are overt, covert, embedded, stark, stereotyped, historical. Our national discussion is a cacophony, not a conversation. Where do I find meaningful dialogues about this fractious issue? How can I counter the sound bites swirling around me? What can I do not to participate in the torrential, inchoate roar that pours through my everyday life, yet still assert my core beliefs in racial equality?

The privilege of my own personal background seems to work against me. When I teach *Huckleberry Finn* or a work by an African-American writer, I must be clear about my own position. Why should I, a white, middle-class academic, raised in an all-white Northern California town; who never saw a black person until the age of 16; whose ethnic horizon was bounded by high school friends named Brunello, Gastaldi and Muskopf; who read about Civil Rights marches in *Time*, nodded appreciatively, and never participated in any late 1960's protest, draft-card burning, sit-in, or march; who basked comfortably in the liberal intellectualization that "of course, all men are created equal; anybody with any sense can understand that—those who contribute to this atmosphere of racism are ignorant and need more effective education"—why should I have the gall to assume some sort of authority to speak to an issue my privilege has protected me from all my life? In fact, these liberal intellectualizations caused me to pay little attention to the complexities of racial discourse until early this century, when the unlikely conjunction of my seminar in Contemporary Literary Theory and my rediscovery of the Prayer of St. Francis gradually began to effect a change. This seemingly contradictory pairing brought me to a place of listening: truly and actively listening to the racialized and ethnicized Other.

Up to that point, during some twenty-five years of teaching, I had the reputation of being a good listener—among students and colleagues both. But the listening was self-concerned: how do I craft my responses to get the return I want? This involved projection. If I say this, will you say that, and if you say something different than I expect, how can I re-craft my further responses to your further responses? In other words, I wasn't truly listening to you; I was trying to anticipate what you would say. Yes, it worked, to some extent, but my underlying motive was to bring you to my position, or, above all, to avoid controversy and contradiction. I had to move away from this habit of mind and conversation to achieve any significant position on race.

Over the years I have taught it, Contemporary Literary Theory has begun to crystallize the concept of the Other in ways I could never have previously considered. Its characterizations of language and discourse involve Post-Structuralism, Postmodernism, Third-Wave Feminism, Critical Race Theory, Cultural Studies and the like (all those "isms" that conservative academics, politicians and pundits who rail against "relativism" abhor). Such approaches tell us, I suggest to my students, that human relations, and the languages that structure them, consist of oppositions. Consider, I observe, the basic binary contrasts that constitute the four major areas of human categorization: male/female, white/black, rich/poor, heterosexual/homosexual. Notice also, I offer to my students, that the first term in these oppositions is the locus of power, authority and ascendancy over the second term—a condition that is historically, economically, politically, culturally and linguistically reinforced. All protest movements, for example, by definition emerge from those rendered subservient and subordinate. Generally speaking (and these oppositions are extremely broad, and many variations and contrasts lurk within these wide boundaries), it is in the interest—even the survival-of the group in power, in ascendancy, to maintain and sustain that authority over its Others, over those who differ from that group. And this centered group has many resources at its disposal to try to ensure the continuing subordination of its Others, the most important of which is the ability to define the Other, to determine what characteristics are the natural traits of that Other race or ethnicity. In the American arena of race, these resources run the gamut from the historical all-encompassing fact of legalized slavery to the current minute, subtle, everyday evocations of stereotype. Attacks on Barack Obama's so-called "elitism," for example, look back in large part to condemnation of the nineteenth-century "uppity" Negro who doesn't know his proper place.

In the simplest terms, then, the Other is he who is not like me, and, as privileged center, I marshal myriad tools of knowledge, discourse and power to define him and concurrently define myself because I am what he is not. I am presence—truth, authority and natural superiority; the Other is absence—falsity, subservience and natural inferiority. In that sentence I am generalizing the "I" and the "he," but the problem is that I, Jay Elliott, am part of the centered, privileged "I." As a member of that center, I have two apparent choices, both of which appropriate the identity of the racialized Other and attempt to erase him. I can support the status quo and implicitly emphasize the racial inferiority of people of color, or I can deny that there is any difference between us. In other words, I can either not be the Other, or I can be the Other. If I attempt not to be the Other, I am marginalizing his unique conditions by refusing to listen at all. If I attempt to be the Other, I am stripping him of his individuality and refusing to listen to his unique conditions by envisioning him according to my own wishes and fears. The novelist Toni Morrison, in her 1992 Harvard lecture "Black Matters," elegantly encapsulates this dilemma, but offers a solution: ". . . [F]or me, imagining is not merely looking or looking at; nor is it taking oneself intact into the other. It is, for the purposes of the work, becoming." Gazing, or "merely looking or looking at," objectifies and dehumanizes both the self and the Other; taking oneself "intact into the other" objectifies and dehumanizes both self and Other in an act of colonization. But "becoming": that opens up an entirely new vista on this issue for me.

Morrison is here specifically addressing readers of literature, but I take her formulation of "becoming" as metaphor for ways I can "read" the life around me—reading as imaginative listening. If I take as my text not simply words within board covers, but the racialized voices and images that stream about me, then Morrison suggests a way of engaging without dehumanizing or objectifying: by listening through my imagination, as it were, I constantly reach towards he who is different. When I acknowledge that difference, moreover, I accept that there is no end point to this empathy, no final horizon where that "becoming" culminates in being identical to that Other. It is a constant process of engagement, of emotional and psychological presence, of negotiation, of active constructive listening and speaking.

But a problem remained: how do I put this theory of "becoming," based as it is on an interpretative strategy directed at reading American literature, into practice? And here is where the Prayer of St. Francis began to come into focus. I had been reacquainting myself with the Prayer when it occurred to me that it was a prayer of becoming.

"Lord, make me an instrument of Thy peace...
grant that I may not so much seek
To be consoled as to console,
To be understood as to understand,

To be loved as to love...."

It is a prayer of reaching out towards all Others; but crucially, it positions the petitioner on an equal basis with those Others. I and you are equally children of God, instruments of faith, and even if I play violin to your oboe and some listeners mistakenly feel that the violin part is naturally more important than the lowly oboe, we are both equally responsible for our participation in the overall harmony, and I know the roles could be reversed.

Thus the Prayer of St. Francis has proved to be the spiritual place on which I could ground the theory. Morrison's formulation provides a junction between a resolutely secular description of the formation of the Other along racial lines and a seemingly impossible-to-attain spirituality. I am no longer implicitly or unconsciously protected by my privilege because I can voluntarily adopt a condition of humility through the prayer, and that humility can, if I practice it fully enough, thread through my everyday life and conversation. Were I not to speak about race, I would be complicit in the now discredited habit that ignoring it is "understood to be a graceful, even generous, liberal gesture," as Morrison says, a state that has the effect of covertly perpetuating white authority through silence. Were I to seize upon those differences that are culturally designated as racial, I would be explicitly supportive of white authority, an overt assertion of black inferiority as the Other. "Becoming," however—reaching out from a place of spiritual humility and serenity to others—facilitates discussion and dialogue. "Let me be an instrument of Thy peace," and let me listen.

# contributors

**tim ahrens**
is Sr. Minister of the First Congregational Church, United Church of Christ, downtown Columbus, Ohio. He is a founding pastor of the BREAD organization and We Believe Ohio. He is a regular contributor to *The Columbus Dispatch* and recently was presented the William Sloane Coffin Award for Justice and Peace by Yale Divinity School. His email is: Tim@first-church.org

**heather powers albanesi**
is an assistant professor at the University of Colorado at Colorado Springs, Colorado. She is currently conducting research on the parental desire for hegemonic masculinity in the 'redshirting' of kindergarteners. She teaches both graduate and undergraduate courses in social theory, sexuality, gender, religion and social class. Heather has 5-year-old twin daughters and a 4-year-old son.

**kimberly broderick**
is a proud-to-be-50-year-old Black woman. Originally from New York City, New York, she now resides in western Massachusetts. She has two amazing sons and is a mentor to a teenage girl. She is a writer, researcher, and observer of the ups and downs of being human.

**sarah buteux**

is an ordained Swedenborgian minister currently serving the First Congregational Church of Hadley, Massachusetts. She lives with her husband and son in Amherst, Massachusetts.

**carole ann camp**

is a Renaissance person, having degrees in science education and Ministry. She is a retired United Church of Christ pastor and has written and published on a variety of topics, including *Praying at Every Turn: Meditations for Walking the Labyrinth*, and co-author with Donna Schaper of *Labyrinths from the Outside In: Walking to Spiritual Insight: A Beginner's Guide*.

**dorothy cresswell**

lives with her partner in western Massachusetts, teaches kindergarten, writes, and makes music in her free time. She was born in the deep south (in Mississippi) and grew up in a community which strove to eliminate traditional divisions. Teaching tolerance is a high priority, both in the classroom and beyond.

**gretchen curry**

grew up in Connecticut. Following high school she served a year as an AmeriCorps Volunteer in San Antonio, Texas. Currently she attends Ohio Wesleyan University where she is a member of the class of 2012.

**susan daniels**

lives in Easthampton, Massachusetts. Her previous stories have centered on her theatrical career, and she credits her years of living in Tennessee as the reason she has played so many Southern women on the stage.

**jay elliott**

is Professor of English at Clark University, Worcester, Massachusetts. Besides teaching American Literature and Introductory Literary Theory, he is now working on the literature of blogs. He also umpires, working occasionally with his son Colin, who attends Renssellaer Polytechnic

Institute.  He lives with his wife, Linda Roghaar, in Amherst, Massachusetts.

## vicki kemper

is pastor of the First Congregational Church, United Church of Christ, in Amherst, Massachusetts. She previously worked as a journalist, writing and editing for the *Los Angeles Times* and other publications. She began writing against racism at her nearly all-white Texas high school, where she was almost expelled for her editorial criticizing the racist actions of fellow students. She lived in Washington, D.C., for 23 years, many of them as the only white person in her working-class, African-American neighborhood.

## hari stephen kumar

retired from engineering at 32 to begin a career in the liberal arts. He is a graduate student at the University of Massachusetts, Amherst, focusing on performance, folklore, and rhetoric. He was born in India in 1976, spent his childhood in Yemen, and has been living in Massachusetts since 1997.

## dusty miller

is a writer and consulting psychologist and the author of numerous articles and four books, including *Women Who Hurt Themselves: Addiction and Trauma Recovery*; *Healing the Body Mind and Spirit*; *Your Surviving Spirit*; and *Stop Running From Love* (2008). She was active in the Civil Rights Movement in the Fayette County voter registration project from 1964–66. This life-changing experience is described in her feature article "The End of Innocence," *Psychotherapy Networker 2004*, (linked on her website dustymiller.org).

## savanna ouellette

is a mediator, a musician, and a lover of books. Lately she is spending a lot of time being a grandma.

**maxine philips**

is moderator of Judson Memorial Church, New York, New York.

**alia starkweather**

began to ask deep, serious questions at a young age. No one gave her good answers to her good questions. As a young adult she attended several churches, trying to "get it." As an older adult she began to read the books that would help create answers. She is still looking for many of the answers. She has been an educator, psychotherapist, caregiver, and is a mother.

**robert stover**

is a civil engineering technician living in Belchertown, Massachusetts.

**marylou sullivan**

is a single mom and the executive director of The Consortium, a not-for-profit agency headquartered in Holyoke, Massachusetts. Check us out at www.wmtcinfo.org—We've got a lot of great things going on! I love to cook, especially impromptu meals for friends. I live in South Amherst, Massachusetts with my sons, Dan (age 20) and Matt (age 13) and our Bichon, Meeko.

**joanne sunshower**

is a consultant and coach for nonprofit professionals and organizations, still believes in the Revolution, and lives next to her grandchildren in Shutesbury, Massachusetts. She has been an organic farmer, a midwife, a teacher, and a chaplain.

**ivy tillman**

is an "on-the-far-side-of-50" African-American, lesbian churchwoman, who lives in Amherst, Massachusetts with her partner and their son. Since she left the south--perhaps for good--in 1966, she has lived in largely white cities and towns. It is not always a comfortable existence, as she has discovered that racism is not "just a southern thang."

**russ vernon-jones**
is a white, heterosexual parent who has been engaged in anti-racism work
with other white folks and in mixed groups for many years. After a career
as a public elementary school teacher and principal, he has recently
moved on to be a consultant and educator, helping people in schools,
churches, and other groups learn about racism and pursue racial justice.
One of his current projects can be viewed at www.anti-racismonline.org.

**james e. wolff**
is the senior pastor at Lawndale Christian Reformed Church. He has
been ministering at this multicultural church in urban Chicago, Illinois,
for more than 25 years. This piece became possible through sabbatical
time from the church, a grant from the Louisville Institute, a writing
workshop at the Collegeville Institute, conversations with Eugene
Peterson, the website at Resources for American Christianity, Martha
and Mark Lipscomb, and the Clinton Taylor family graciously inviting
Jim into their story.

# copyright

Printed in the United States
207568BV00001B/166-267/P

9 781935 052111